Karate-Do
Foundations

Mark R. Moeller

MASTERS PRESS

A division of Howard W. Sams & Co.

Published by Masters Press (A Division of Howard W. Sams & Co.)
2647 Waterfront Pkwy. E. Dr. Suite 300
Indianapolis, IN 46214

Published 1995
Printed in the United States of America

Library of Congress Cataloging-in Publication Data

Moeller, Mark R., 1960-
　　　Karate-do foundations / Mark R. Moeller.
　　　　　　　　p.　　　cm.
　　　Includes index.
　　　ISBN 1-57028-026-6 (pbk.)
　　　1. Karate.　I. Title.
　　GV1114.3.M64　1995　　　　　　　　　　　95-10017
　　796.8'153--dc20　　　　　　　　　　　　　　CIP

The author and publisher assume no responsibility for any injury that may occur as a result of attempting to do any of the movements, techniques, or exercises described in this book or using any of the movements and techniques against another person. Neither the author nor the publisher makes any warranty or guarantee that any of the materials described will be effective against an attacker, in a self-defense situation, or otherwise. The reader should consult a physician before attempting any of the materials described in this book.

FOREWORD

Okinawan Karate has become famous as a means by which a weaker or unarmed person can defeat a stronger or armed opponent. However, the exact nature of the traditional martial arts curriculum, which makes such accomplishments possible, is less well-known. This is unfortunate, but inevitable because of the emphasis in the martial arts community and society at large on ostentatious and superficial physical techniques at the expense of attention to the fundamental principles that lead to positive character development. It is no surprise then, in an era when martial arts are too often practiced as sport and entertainment, that character development is often neglected.

In contrast to popular misconceptions, the essential philosophy of the Okinawan Martial Arts is that physical technique can ultimately be no better than the character of the individual. This is the basic difference between Budo, the Way of the Martial Artist, and the emphasis on physical technique alone that too often characterizes the pursuit of martial sport. This does not mean that physical technique is inconsequential. Indeed, the doctrine of the traditional martial arts cannot be revealed except through the diligent practice of physical technique.

The importance of Mark Moeller's new book is that it will enable the beginning or advanced student to pursue his or her physical training in a manner that facilitates character development in accordance with the fundamental principles of Budo. Never before has a book explicating the basics of Okinawan Karate been available in English in such an accessible form, and Mark Moeller is admirably suited to rectify this situation. With continuous training beginning in the late seventies, certifications in special instructors' programs, years of teaching experience and exposure to top exponents of the martial arts from both the United States and East Asia, he is well qualified to present in writing the basic teachings of the system.

Most importantly, Mr. Moeller's success in his personal life and chosen career in law exemplifies the most important principle in all traditional martial arts: Sincerity in training leads not only to success in the confines of the training hall, but to success and integrity in one's life as a whole. Personal development — not simply in the limited sphere of physical technique, but in the ultimately more significant respects of personal growth and contribution to society as a whole — is a true value of training in the martial arts. It is to this goal that this book can contribute.

Karl W. Scott III
Branch Director
Kokusai Budoin
IMAF/USA
Executive Director
Asian Martial Arts Studio
Ann Arbor, Michigan

DEDICATION

To my wife, Sharon, and my daughter, Jennifer, for their patient love and
support of my martial arts training.

TABLE OF CONTENTS

ACKNOWLEDGMENTS

My parents, Robert and Mary Ann Moeller, for always loving me and encouraging me to learn and grow.

I would like to thank my teachers and my students for all they have taught me and all they continue to teach me.

For editorial assistance, I am grateful to Karl W. Scott III; Y. Jay Sandweiss; Scott Schwahn; Tim Cox; David Crane; Bradford Clancy; Mark Taylor; Mark Snepp; Nicklaus Suino; Herb Goldberg; my sister, Michelle Kasprisin; my parents, Robert and Mary Ann Moeller; and especially my wife, Sharon.

All photos were taken by Susan Bennett. Special thanks to Susan for all her hard work.

For their participation and assistance with the photos, I am indebted to my students — Scott Schwahn, Mark Snepp, David Crane, Joni Vance, Tim Cox, Chip Abernathy, and Mark Taylor.

Special thanks to Sharon Brown for her wordprocessing assistance in the preparation of the initial drafts of this book.

Thanks to Melody Moore and David Rosenbaum for their advice and assistance with computers and computer graphics.

I am also indebted to Nicklaus Suino for advice and assistance with the securing of a publisher and for assistance with Japanese terminology and pronunciation.

I am also grateful for the assistance of Karl W. Scott III and the Asian Martial Arts Studio in connection with the preparation of historical data and biographical information. The charts in the chapter entitled My Teachers of Shobayashi Shorin Ryu and Shudokan Karate-Do were prepared by the Asian Martial Arts Studio and are used with permission.

The original design concept for the cover was the idea of Tim Cox. The Japanese calligraphy was done by H.E. Davey and it reads: *Karate-do Kihon*. This means Karate-do Foundations or Karate-do Fundamentals. I appreciate their help.

CREDITS

Cover design and diagrams — Suzanne Lincoln
Editor — Heather Seal
Production assistance — Terry Varvel
Proofreader — Pat Brady

INTRODUCTION

The study of traditional Okinawan Karate-do has had a significant impact on my life. Not only have I learned how to defend myself, but also how to succeed in all areas of my life. It can make the same difference in your life.

This book is a product of my desire to share karate with as many people as possible and to preserve the important principles, techniques, and exercises of traditional Okinawan Karate-do. Because karate has given so much to me, I have always felt a strong desire to give something back by sharing with others the things that I have learned. Over the past 12 years, I have accomplished this primarily by teaching others. It gives me great joy and satisfaction to see others learn and grow through their practice of karate.

For years my students have asked if there were any books that would help them practice and remember the techniques and exercises they learned in class. Until now, I have always had to answer that there were no such books.

This book is a detailed training and instruction manual for those who wish to learn traditional Okinawan Karate-do or to improve their existing karate skills. The text and illustrations explain traditional Okinawan Karate-do in the effective, time-proven method that I use to teach new students in my classes. This systematic progression is the way I learned karate from my teachers, Y. Jay Sandweiss Sensei and Karl W. Scott III Sensei. (*Sensei* is the Japanese word for teacher, and in Japanese it always follows the teacher's name.)

Learning karate was not easy for me. In order to learn karate, I had to continually break down the techniques and exercises into their simplest movements. I then practiced these movements over and over again until I learned them well enough to combine them back into the original technique or exercise. In this book, I have done the same thing. The techniques and exercises have been broken down and described in great detail to make them easier to learn.

This book was written for students at all levels (from beginner to advanced) and as a resource for instructors. Although the techniques and exercises described in this book are the ones that I teach to beginning students in my classes, they are not just for "beginners." Rather, it is important that practitioners at all levels of karate continue practicing these exercises so that the key techniques become so ingrained in the practitioner that they are second nature and are performed instinctively. In addition the "basics," which are the most important principles and techniques, are contained in these exercises. Without a firm understanding of these principles and the ability to execute these techniques, practitioners will not be able to reach their maximum potential.

This book was also written for students and teachers of other styles of karate. The techniques and exercises can be used to supplement and enhance your current training. It will also increase your understanding of the key principles and techniques of effective karate. Although there are many different styles and variations of karate, there are key principles and techniques that apply to every style. This book describes many of those key principles and techniques.

For those individuals who do not have the opportunity to train with me or my teachers, this book is a guide to the principles of karate as well as specific techniques involved in training. While no book can take the place of a qualified instructor, you can begin to learn karate by practicing these materials. The explanation of the key principles will help you to understand and improve your execution of the specific techniques. The principles can also help you find an instructor because they will give you a basis for evaluating instructors. Qualified instructors will apply these principles in their execution of similar techniques. The best instructors will also explain the principles behind their techniques so students will be able to execute the techniques in the most effective manner and understand the essence of the techniques.

I also wanted to preserve in print traditional Okinawan Karate-do. To my knowledge, there are no other books in English that describe the Shobayashi Shorin Ryu system of Karate-do taught by Grandmaster Eizo Shimabukuro or the Shudokan system of Karate-do created by the late Grandmaster Kanken Toyama. These 10th degree black belts (10th *dans*) devoted their lives to the teaching of traditional Okinawan Karate-do and have students throughout the world. The Shudokan system is also taught under the name of Doshinkan Karate-do in Europe and America by Isao Ichikawa Sensei. Grandmaster Ichikawa Sensei was one of Grandmaster Toyama's senior students who was promoted to 10th *dan* by Grandmaster Toyama.

Finally, this book is a tribute to my teachers, Y. Jay Sandweiss Sensei and Karl W. Scott III Sensei, and to their teachers, Herbert Z. Wong Sensei and Walter E. Todd Sensei. It summarizes the principles, techniques, and exercises that I have learned from them. I do not take credit for discovering any of the principles or creating any of the techniques and exercises described in this book. Rather, I have worked hard to accurately describe them and to present them in a format that is easy to learn.

The study of traditional Okinawan Karate-do will teach you how to succeed in self-defense situations as well as in other areas of your life. I am confident that you will find this book a valuable resource and aid for both.

Read this book carefully. Learn and practice the techniques and exercises. Strive to fully understand the principles and then apply them during each practice session. One must continue to practice and practice. This is the only way to learn karate. There are no short cuts or easy ways. It is only through repetition that the principles and techniques may be learned and internalized. With this repeated practice, the body itself will absorb and learn the principles and techniques.

OVERVIEW

This book is divided into two parts. Part I describes Shobayashi Shorin Ryu and Shudokan Karate-do, the traditional systems of Okinawan Karate-do from which the techniques and exercises originated. It also describes my own insights and experiences in the martial arts. Part I ends with a section describing the training history and some notable experiences of my teachers. Part II is the technical portion of the book. It explains and illustrates the techniques, exercises and principles of these systems of Okinawan Karate-do.

Part I begins by describing the origins and major emphases of the Shobayashi Shorin Ryu and Shudokan systems of Karate-do. It also contains information about Eizo Shimabukuro, the current Grandmaster of Shobayashi Shorin Ryu, and the late Kanken Toyama, the founder and Grandmaster of Shudokan.

After the sections on the systems, Part I discusses why one should learn the specific techniques and exercises described in this book and the importance of continuing to practice them. These fundamental techniques are critical to the development of a strong karate foundation. This foundation forms the base for the development of all subsequent karate skills. Karate is like a building in this respect: it can never be stronger than the foundation. In order to become proficient in karate, one must therefore concentrate on these basics and continually strive to improve them.

The next sections describe some of the benefits that can be derived from karate. In addition to the benefits of learning to defend oneself, these benefits also include how to effectively set and achieve goals, how to increase concentration, how to more efficiently focus mental and physical energy, and how to remain calm in threatening situations. It will become clear that the study of karate provides considerably more than just self-defense benefits. The principles and skills learned from karate can be applied to all areas of life.

Part I continues with an explanation of the development of karate "reflexes." My own term for this phenomenon is "body knowledge." A person has developed body knowledge of karate when his or her body instinctively and unconsciously executes the appropriate karate techniques in response to an attack or a dangerous situation. Quality training and repetitions are the key factors in the development of body knowledge.

The next section contains historical information and stories about my teachers. These men are all exceptional martial artists and teachers. They have devoted substantial portions of their lives to the development of their own martial skills and guiding the development of others' martial skills. I have included this information both as a tribute to them and as an inspiration for you. The path of the martial artist is not an easy one. It requires practice, perseverance, and patience. Without this kind of personal sacrifice and dedication, one cannot develop effective martial skills. These stories will help motivate you to continue in your own training even when things do not seem to be going well.

Part I ends with recommendations on how to learn karate and get the most out of this book. If you follow these recommendations, you will learn the basics of karate in a very efficient and effective manner. These recommendations can also be applied to other physical activities or sports to enhance your abilities.

The remainder of the book explains and illustrates the technical aspects of karate. Part II begins with important protocol, body positions, stances, and stationary techniques. It explains the individual components and key principles necessary to develop strong stances, powerful punches, effective blocks, and explosive kicks. These techniques are the building blocks for the development of effective karate skills.

Part II then describes individual exercises that link the techniques together in a moving context. These exercises provide a systematic way to learn and practice these building blocks. In addition to describing the proper way to execute these techniques and exercises, these chapters also explain the underlying principles which are necessary for strong and effective techniques. If a particular principle is understood, it may be used to enhance the effectiveness of hundreds of other techniques. Knowing these principles will also help you to understand the important elements of the exercises and techniques as well as the benefits to be derived from them.

The Two-Person Exercises that follow apply the techniques and skills learned from the individual exercises to a variety of attacks. They also teach essential skills related to timing, rhythm and distancing. The Two-Person Exercises are done slowly in the beginning to establish rhythm and control. The speed is then gradually increased until they can be executed at full speed with good control.

The final chapters of Part II present three *Taikyuka Kata* which combine specific techniques and teach methods of generating power. (In Japanese there are no plural words so *kata* can refer to one or more *kata*.) *Kata* represent the culmination of a practitioner's individual training. As one progresses, almost all of one's individual training is spent practicing *kata*. Many *kata* have been passed down for hundreds of years and often contain the heart of a particular system's karate.

Kata practice also teaches how to enter into the mental state known as *mushin* or "no-mind." *Mushin* reduces the involvement of the conscious mind, and this enables the practitioner to more effectively utilize the intuitive knowledge of the entire mind. After the ability to enter this mental state has been learned in individual practice, it can be applied in two-person situations. When this is done, the trained practitioner instinctively reacts in the quickest and most appropriate manner to an attack.

KARATE-DO
FOUNDATIONS

PART I

SHOBAYASHI SHORIN RYU AND SHUDOKAN KARATE-DO

The techniques and exercises in this book are from the Shobayashi Shorin Ryu and the Shudokan systems of Okinawan Karate-do. This section will provide a brief description of the two systems, Grandmaster Eizo Shimabukuro and Grandmaster Kanken Toyama.

Shorin Ryu is one of the three main systems of Okinawan Karate-do and can be traced back to the 1400s. (The other main systems are Goju Ryu and the now extinct Tomari-te.) The name "Shorin Ryu Karate-do" may be translated as "The Shaolin System of the Way of the Empty Hand."

The word "Way" (*Do*) means the path one follows through life and is called the *Tao* in Chinese. It is used in the names of many martial arts to indicate that practitioners are learning the moral and philosophical aspects of the art in addition to the physical techniques. For the serious practitioner, the study of Karate-do is a way of life.

Shorin Ryu developed as a combination of various Chinese martial arts and indigenous fighting techniques of the Okinawan people. It is one of the oldest and most traditional styles of Okinawan Karate-do. Shobayashi Shorin Ryu was organized by Master Chotoku Kiyan, and the current Grandmaster is Grandmaster Eizo Shimabukuro. The Shobayashi Shorin Ryu system emphasizes straight-line techniques, angular attacking, and quick stepping to move inside and outside of an opponent's defenses. It teaches a practitioner how to use the body as an integrated whole to generate explosive power.

The Shudokan system was created in the 1930's by Grandmaster Kanken Toyama. The name "Shudokan Karate-do" may be translated as "The Institute for the Cultivation of the Way of the Empty Hand." Grandmaster Toyama was a master of many styles of Okinawan Karate-do. He incorporated techniques, exercises and *kata* from all the major systems of Okinawan Karate-do, including Shorin Ryu. He also created exercises and *kata* that are unique to the Shudokan system. Shudokan emphasizes large, circular motions, covering techniques, and deep, narrow stances. It teaches the practitioner how to use whipping motions and the expansion and contraction of different muscles to generate a type of power that is like waves crashing on a beach.

The Shobayashi Shorin Ryu and Shudokan systems of Okinawan Karate-do compliment each other very well. Shobayashi Shorin Ryu emphasizes more straight-line motions and techniques, while Shudokan emphasizes more circular motions and techniques. Shobayashi Shorin Ryu incorporates many upright stances that provide great mobility, while Shudokan emphasizes deep stances that provide a strong foundation. There are also many techniques that are the same in both systems. The practice of the techniques and exercises from these two systems provides a balanced and diversified training program for the development of karate skills.

GRANDMASTER EIZO SHIMABUKURO (b. 1925)

Grandmaster Shimabukuro (Shimabukuro is a more formal way of saying Shimabuku) started training in Goju Ryu as a young boy. His teachers included Chojun Miyagi, Choki Motobu and Tatsuo Shimabuku, his older brother and founder of the Isshin Ryu system. At the age of 16, he started training in Shorin Ryu with Grandmaster Chotoku Kiyan. Grandmaster Kiyan was known for his jumping and kicking ability. His fighting style emulated the strategies and techniques of a fighting cock. Master Kiyan would often attack an opponent's extremities, and he relied on quick stepping to move in to attack his opponent and then retreat before the opponent could counterattack. Grandmaster Shimabukuro was chosen to be the Grandmaster and successor to the Shobayashi branch of Shorin Ryu by Grandmaster Kiyan.

In 1959 at the age of 34, Grandmaster Shimabukuro became the youngest person ever to receive a 10th dan. His 10th dan was awarded by Grandmaster Kanken Toyama and his certificate is No. 25. Grandmaster Toyama also made him the Chairman of the Okinawan branch of the All Japan Karate-do League.

GRANDMASTER KANKEN TOYAMA (1888 - 1966)

Grandmaster Kanken Toyama, whose Okinawan name was Kanken Oyadamari, was an Okinawan karate master who moved to Japan after Gichin Funakoshi's introduction of karate in the early 1920s. He started his karate training at age nine with a master named Itarashiki. Although he studied under many different Okinawan Karate-do masters (including Aragaki, Azato, Chibana, Higaona, Oshiro, and Tana), his primary teacher was Master Yasutsune Itosu. Grandmaster Toyama was one of Master Itosu's top students, and he became one of Master Itosu's senior instructors in 1907. He studied under Master Itosu for 18 years and was one of only two of Itosu's students to be granted the title *Shihanchi*, or protege, of Master Itosu's *O kuge* (Innermost secrets). Grandmaster Toyama was known for his strong gripping techniques and his incorporation of lion and tiger techniques in his karate. The Japanese government gave Grandmaster Toyama the title of "Master Instructor" and the authority to award 10th dans in any system of Okinawan or Japanese Karate-do.

THE IMPORTANCE OF THE BASICS
or
THE PATH OF INTERLOCKING CIRCLES

The process of continually working on the basics can be described as a path of interlocking circles which a person must follow in order to progress in karate. When a person starts studying karate (or any other sport or physical activity), one can imagine that the person is at the very bottom of a small imaginary circle. Here the person learns the core techniques, exercises, and principles of karate. These basics provide the foundation for all subsequent development and are the most important elements.

As the person practices these fundamental techniques of karate and progresses, there is upward movement along the left side of the imaginary circle until the person reaches the top of the first circle (See Illustration 1). At this point, the person is ready to learn more and begins to work on more advanced materials. In order to progress in the quickest and most efficient way, the person needs to practice the new materials while continuing to practice the basics. This

continued practicing of the basics is a return to the starting point. This can be visualized as a movement downward along the right side of the imaginary circle and back to the starting point at the bottom of the circle. At this starting point, work continues simultaneously on both the new and the old materials. As the person's execution of the basics improves, the person finds that the execution of the newer and more advanced materials also improves.

The path then continues as the person moves upward along the left side of a second imaginary circle. This second circle has the same starting point as the first circle (which is why they are called interlocking circles), but it is a larger circle. When the person reaches the top of this second, larger circle, the person is at a level which is higher than the top of the previous circle (See Illustration 2). At this point, the person is ready to begin learning more advanced materials. Again, the person must continue to work

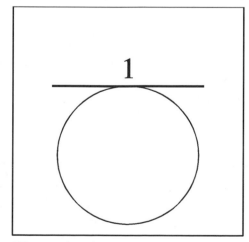

Illustration 1

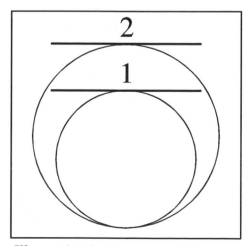

Illustration 2

on improving the basics while practicing the more advanced materials, thereby returning along the right side of the larger circle to the starting point.

As the basics and more advanced materials improve, the person again moves upward along the left side of an even larger circle and the process is repeated. Illustration 3 is a visual representation of the path of the interlocking circles. There is no limit to the number of times the circular process can be repeated or the level of proficiency that may be reached. The only limiting factor is the person's willingness to repeatedly return to the starting point and work on improving his or her execution of the basics in addition to practicing more advanced materials.

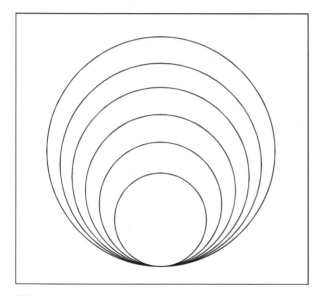

Illustration 3

The path of the interlocking circles is one reason why karate instructors continue to progress to higher levels of proficiency even when they do not practice with peers or train with a teacher. The following personal story illustrates this point and the importance of practicing the basics.

I left my karate teachers in 1983 when I moved to North Carolina to attend law school. Within a few weeks of starting law school, I started my first karate school — the Asian Martial Arts Club at Duke University. When I graduated in 1986, I moved to Atlanta and started my current school — Atlanta's Traditional Okinawan Karate-do Dojo. In early 1988, I was told I would be testing for my 2nd dan with another student on my next trip to Ann Arbor, Michigan.

Although I had continued to visit and train with my teachers a few times every year, almost all of my training had been done with my students. One problem I faced in preparing for the test was that none of my students were advanced enough to practice most of the two-person exercises required for the test. Because there was nothing I could do about this, I decided to concentrate on practicing the basics and the individual materials required for the test. In addition, I also repeatedly practiced the two-person exercises described in this book.

The test was held on April 22, 1988. It went well, and my friend and I both received our 2nd dan. After the test, I received a somewhat unusual compliment that I still treasure. The compliment came from one of the senior Aikido students (who had also studied a number of other martial arts during his 20-plus years of martial arts training). He said that he did not want me to take his comments the wrong way, but he was surprised at how well I did on the test. Because I had been gone for five years while my friend had continued to train closely with Scott Sensei, he had expected to see a big difference between us. Despite my absence, he said that he had not seen a noticeable difference in our execution of the various materials or our relative level of proficiency.

I thanked him for his compliment and explained how I had decided to concentrate on the basics in order to prepare for the test. We also discussed the amount of time I had spent over the five-year period teaching the basics to new students and practicing those techniques and exercises with them. In looking back on this experience, I realized that it validates the path of the interlocking circles and shows the importance of continuing to practice the basics.

BENEFITS OF KARATE TRAINING

Before beginning the technical portion of this book, I want to share some of the benefits that I have derived from my karate training. In particular, I want to discuss some of the non-martial benefits. Most people realize that karate training effectively teaches people how to defend themselves, but many are unaware of the other skills and abilities that are developed. These other skills and abilities enhance the martial effectiveness of the practitioner's karate. They also provide the practitioner with the inner resources and skills to succeed in other areas of life.

The principles that I have learned from my teachers and my karate training have taught me how to achieve success in karate and in life. I have learned how to set realistic goals, how to develop the necessary self-discipline to follow through on these goals, and how to maintain the most productive attitude while working toward these goals. These principles are a very effective and efficient way to successfully accomplish any goal.

The practice of karate has also greatly increased my ability to concentrate and has taught me how to focus my mental and physical energy. I have also learned the importance of practicing something over and over until it is learned. By applying these principles in my karate training and in my life, my self-confidence has increased and I have done things I never dreamed possible.

This has not been an easy process. With respect to karate, it has required hundreds of thousands of hours of repetitions and practice. With respect to other areas of my life, it has often required an equivalent amount of hard work and patience. My efforts have been rewarded, however, and I have successfully achieved many of my goals in life. There are other goals that I am still working on, but I continue to apply these principles and am confident that I will eventually succeed. The following describes how I discovered and applied these principles in my karate training.

I was a slow learner when it came to karate. In high school, I was a fairly talented athlete. I played on my school's football, basketball, baseball, and tennis teams. Although I was never a superstar, I was generally a starter. Nevertheless, when I started studying karate at the University of Michigan Shorin Ryu Karate-do Club in January of 1979, I found that I had great difficulty getting my body to properly execute the techniques and exercises I learned in class. In fact, I frequently had to ask the other students to slow down just so I could do the two-person exercises. Because of the caliber of person the class attracted, the other students were always very helpful and supportive.

I soon realized that just attending the two classes offered each week was not enough for me to learn karate. I decided I would try to practice at least once every weekend. I began doing this and found that the extra practice helped considerably. Although there was not a dramatic improvement in my ability to do karate, I was encouraged by the results of this extra practice. In small increments, I gradually increased the number of practice sessions until I was practicing every day for one to two hours (with only an occasional day missed).

Despite my daily practice, however, I was still one of the slowest learners in the class. At the end of that first semester, twelve out of the fifteen students in the class tested for their first promotion. I was one of the students who was not asked to test. (In many traditional martial arts schools, a student cannot test for a promotion until asked by the Sensei. It is considered improper and disrespectful to ask to test. When the Sensei feels a student is ready, the student is invited to test for promotion.)

I wanted to learn karate, however, so I did not allow myself to get frustrated and upset. Instead, I persevered and continued my daily practice. Within six months, I tested and received my first promotion. It is interesting to note that within one year all twelve of the students who participated in that first test were no longer training, and the three of us who did not participate in that test all went on to get our black belts.

In this process, I discovered that if I practiced a particular technique or exercise enough times, I would eventually learn how to do it correctly. From that point on, I have continued to train daily — sometimes training for as many as eight hours a day. Consistent practice and multiple repetitions have been, and continue to be, two of the keys to my success in karate.

Although I was not conscious of this at the time, I later realized that I had learned how to work toward achieving any goal and how to apply the principles of effective goal setting. I started with a clear picture of the end result I wanted to achieve. (My ultimate goal was to earn a black belt in karate.) I then established an intermediate goal that would move me closer to achieving my ultimate goal. This intermediate goal was specific and realistic. It also contained a component that was capable of being "measured" so I could determine whether I had successfully completed it. (As described above, my first intermediate goal was to practice at least once every weekend.)

After I successfully achieved my first intermediate goal, I revised that goal and set another intermediate goal that would move me closer to achieving my ultimate goal. (I increased the number of weekly practice sessions and created subgoals to determine which exercises to practice during those sessions.) I continued to repeat this process of setting realistic goals, working hard to achieve them, and then revising them, over and over again. I persevered and continued working even during times when it looked like I might never achieve my ultimate goal.

My perseverance paid off. Gradually, I became more and more proficient in karate and eventually earned my black belt. (The black belt I was presented originally belonged to Scott Sensei. He presented it to Sandweiss Sensei immediately before leaving for extended martial arts training in California. Scott Sensei had chosen Sandweiss Sensei to be the Acting Head Instructor while he was gone. At the time, he told Sandweiss Sensei that it was a "Head Instructor's Belt" and that he should wear it until he had the right student to pass it on to. I feel very honored that I was the one chosen to receive this belt. I received the same instructions about the belt and passed it on when the right student earned it.) In the process, I also revised my original ultimate goal to include training for the rest of my life and sharing Okinawan Karate-do with others.

These are the key principles for achieving success in any endeavor. One needs a clear picture of the desired result, intermediate steps (with revisions as necessary) to move closer to the desired result, and the perseverance to continue working toward the desired result.

Because perseverance is both the most important and the most difficult aspect of achieving one's goals, I want to share my insights on the attitude one should maintain when working toward the achievement of any goal. Mental and physical energy should not be wasted worrying about the end result, the rate of progress, or the proficiency level or successes of others. Rather, the mind and all of one's energy should be focused on doing those things that are necessary to achieve the goal. This is both effective and efficient. It also leads to greater peace of mind and internal harmony because one knows that he or she is on the path to success and is doing all that can be done. In my opinion, this is the most productive attitude that one can have when working toward the achievement of any goal.

For example, I wanted to learn how to do a middle block during the first semester of my karate training. Instead of focusing on the block itself and my inability to do it properly, I focused my mind and energy on practicing the block. I did not worry about how fast I was progressing or how I compared to the other students. These factors were not in my control. What I could control was the number of repetitions I did and how hard I tried during each repetition. I started by doing ten blocks each day and gradually increased the number of repetitions until I reached the maximum number I could complete in my allotted practice time. During each repetition, I concentrated on executing the block to the best of my ability. Gradually over time, I learned how to do a good middle block. I then reduced the number of repetitions to a "maintenance" level and chose a different technique to practice. Gradually, I learned the required techniques and exercises of karate.

In addition to enabling me to learn faster and more efficiently, focusing on the number of repetitions and the quality of each repetition (instead of the rate of progress or my proficiency compared to others) also prevented me from getting frustrated with myself. This is not to say that there were not times when I wished I was learning faster, but at least I knew that I was on the correct pathway. I was doing everything I could to ensure that I learned the techniques and exercises. This is the attitude or mental outlook that one should maintain when working toward the achievement of any goal.

The study of karate has also improved my self-confidence. My increased confidence is a result of the self-defense skills I have learned and the improvement I have witnessed in myself. I feel good about myself and what I have accomplished in my life. I know I have the inner resources and skills to meet the challenges that life throws at me and the courage to attempt things that seem unattainable at first. I have found that many of these things eventually turn out to be not only attainable, but also worth the effort to attain them.

Goal Setting in Life

I have also applied the principles of setting realistic goals, working diligently to achieve them, and maintaining a productive attitude while working toward these goals to many areas of my life besides karate training. For example, one of my goals in life was to become an attorney like my father. In order to become an attorney, one must complete seven years of college after completing high school. I studied hard in college to maintain the grades that would be necessary to reach this goal. When it came time to take the LSAT (the national test required by law schools for admission), I studied at least four hours a day for three months and did well. I was accepted by a number of law schools and ultimately chose Duke University because of its excellent reputation and the scholarship they offered me.

I started law school in the fall of 1983 and, shortly thereafter, achieved another goal I had set for myself. Despite the rigors of law school, I started my first karate school — the Asian Martial Arts Club at Duke University — during my first semester so I could share with others the knowledge and benefits I had received. Throughout law school, I taught karate classes three times a week and continued my own personal training on the other days of the week.

I continued to apply the principles I had learned from karate to both my teaching and my school work. My karate school grew from five to thirty-five students over the three years of law school. My grades were good enough to enable me to make the law review staff of *Law & Contemporary Problems* at Duke University and to graduate with honors.

I graduated from law school in 1986 and moved to Atlanta, Georgia. I passed the Georgia bar exam and achieved my goal of becoming an attorney. Within a year of my move to Atlanta, I started my current school — Atlanta's Traditional Okinawan Karate-do Dojo. I continue to teach karate classes three times a week and practice almost everyday.

These are just a few examples of the successes I have achieved as a result of the goal setting principles I learned from karate. If you apply these principles of goal setting and working hard, you can learn karate or succeed in any endeavor you choose.

Focusing Mental and Physical Energy

As one can begin to see, karate offers many benefits and is not just a physical discipline. The mental component is critical. Karate training has increased my concentration and has taught me how to focus both my mental and physical energy.

In order to improve one's execution of karate techniques, a practitioner must think about a number of different things while practicing. For example, the position and movement of one's feet, knees, hips, shoulders, arms and head are all very important. In order to coordinate all these body parts, the practitioner cannot be distracted or allow his or her mind to wander. The mind's attention must be focused on only the particular technique or exercise being practiced at that time. By consistently doing this during practice sessions, the practitioner learns to concentrate intensely. The goal is to use all of one's mental and physical energy to improve the execution of each technique or exercise.

The ability to concentrate intensely and focus one's mental and physical energy develops gradually. It starts as something that occurs without conscious control, but over time and with practice, it can be done at will.

This is an extremely important skill to develop. In a combat situation, it can be the difference between victory and defeat. If the mind is distracted, a person cannot respond and react as effectively. The person's reactions and responses are more likely to be inappropriate or too slow because of the distractions caused by his or her own mind. Karate training teaches the practitioner how to concentrate all of his or her mental and physical energy on the situation. This gives the practitioner the greatest potential for success against an attack.

The ability to concentrate intensely and focus one's mental and physical energy also has a number of non-martial benefits. Because the mind of the karate practitioner is completely engrossed in the improvement of his or her techniques during practice sessions, this time becomes a mental oasis from the stresses of the world. The thoughts, worries, and other concerns of the mind are replaced by an intense focus on karate. This leads to a feeling of mental refreshment during and after practice sessions.

Another benefit of this ability is that one becomes more efficient in the performance of both mental and physical tasks. The mind's focus can be directed toward the completion of any task. This allows a person to complete the particular task in less time than it would take if the mind was wandering off and thinking about other things. It also frequently results in a better finished product or result.

For example, the ability to concentrate intensely and focus my mental and physical energy was a significant advantage to me when I was in college. It enabled me to study more effectively than I could before learning this skill. In addition to being able to study more efficiently during study sessions, I was also able to take advantage of short periods of time that I previously wasted. If I had only twenty minutes between classes, I would use this time to study. I would concentrate all my mind and energy on the work I had to do and block out other distractions. By doing this, I found I could accomplish a significant amount during these short time periods.

My enhanced concentration skills and ability to focus my mental and physical energy also enabled me to do well in school. Despite the fact that I worked seven hours a week at my church (in exchange for lodgings), waited tables at a local restaurant two nights a week, and spent four to five hours almost every day practicing karate and other martial arts, I made the Dean's List every semester in college and graduated with honors from the University of Michigan's English Honors Program. In addition, by the time I was a junior in college, I was able to become financially independent from my parents as a result of merit scholarships and the income earned from my two jobs.

I continue to use this ability in my daily life. As a commercial real estate attorney, I am frequently interrupted by others throughout the day. I also have to work on many different matters at the same time. In order to accomplish my client's objectives and complete my work, I concentrate all my mental energy on one task at a time. When I complete that task or need to work on something else, I switch my mental focus to the next task. This has enabled me to complete all my tasks in an efficient and effective manner.

Remaining Calm in the Face of Danger

Karate training has also taught me how to remain calm in threatening or dangerous situations. Learning how to remain calm in these situations was, and continues to be, an integral part of karate training.

The emphasis in karate on unarmed techniques developed on the island of Okinawa primarily as a result of the conquering of Okinawa by Japanese forces over four hundred years ago. After conquering Okinawa, the Japanese confiscated all the weapons on Okinawa. The practice of karate was also made illegal, so all training had to be done in secret. During this time period, the native Okinawans had to defend themselves against Japanese samurai who were armed with weapons and against local bandits. The skill of the practitioner often determined whether the practitioner lived or died.

It was critical that a person remained calm and used his or her full mental powers during any confrontation with an opponent. The exercises that the Okinawan Karate-do masters developed over the years were designed to include mental training and to teach practitioners how to remain calm in dangerous situations. These exercises have been preserved and are still an integral part of traditional karate training today. One important aspect of these exercises is that they teach practitioners how to be more courageous. Courage develops as practitioners gain confidence in their ability to successfully defend themselves against an attacker. The combination of courage and martial skills developed through karate training teaches practitioners how to remain calm in dangerous situations.

This is still an important skill today. When one allows oneself to get angry or when one is afraid, it is very difficult to think clearly. The mind becomes clouded as the emotions take over the conscious mind. By training the mind to remain calm, one's full mental powers can be directed to the issues at hand in the particular situation. One can then make better decisions and find more creative solutions to problems and conflicts that arise. If a conflict cannot be peaceably resolved, one can also react and defend oneself more effectively when the mind is clear.

It is important to realize that courage is a "learned" trait. Courage comes from training the mind and body to act according to the will despite feelings of fear. The Two-Person Exercises (*Ippon Kumite*) described in this book provide an excellent opportunity to learn and practice courage. To emphasize the development of courage, these exercises can be done without the defender blocking the attack. Courage is developed by learning not to flinch or pull away as one partner executes a full-force technique that is stopped within an inch of the other partner's body. This same type of courage can then be applied when blocking the attack during the regular practice of the Two-Person Exercises. With repeated practice, the practitioner's courage increases and he or she learns how to remain calm in any threatening or dangerous situations.

The ability to remain calm in threatening situations has served me well in other areas of my life. As a commercial real estate attorney, an important part of my job is negotiating on behalf of my clients. My clients have frequently commented on my ability to remain calm even in the most heated negotiations. They are impressed by my ability to keep my emotions under control and not allow others to upset or intimidate me. When they have commented on this ability, I tell them that it is a skill I learned from my karate training.

BODY KNOWLEDGE — DEVELOPING KARATE REFLEXES

A key goal of karate training is to know the techniques so well that they become an automatic response. This response becomes as natural and effortless as breathing or walking. My own name for this phenomenon is "body knowledge."

Body knowledge transcends the conscious mind. It is like a reflex action. When the principles and techniques have been practiced enough to develop this body knowledge, the mind instinctively causes the muscles, bones, tendons, and ligaments to execute them without conscious thought. This feels like the body is responding and reacting by itself. The body naturally executes the appropriate techniques easily, effortlessly, and effectively. This reaction and response also occurs without the time delay or interference of conscious thoughts.

How do you know if you have developed this kind of body knowledge? One option would be to actively seek out and instigate real-life tests by frequently starting fights. This is dangerous for both parties involved, however, and contrary to the philosophical underpinnings of Okinawan Karate-do — namely, that karate should be used only for self-defense and only as a last resort.

Another way to test for body knowledge is the use of surprise attacks. This is a training method developed by the karate masters of old and passed down from teachers to students for centuries. This form of training almost always takes place outside of formal classes and training areas. The sensei waits for a moment when the student is not expecting an attack and then suddenly executes a punch, kick, or strike that stops within an inch of the student's body if it is not blocked. The student who fails to block the attack knows that he would have been struck if the sensei had been executing a real attack.

These surprise attacks are sporadic and infrequent. The sensei, undoubtedly because of his or her own experience and skill level, always seems to know when the student is least expecting a surprise attack. It is only then that the sensei attacks. The surprise attacks continue (generally over a period of years) until the student has developed sufficient body knowledge to successfully block an attack. Once this occurs, the student has passed this "test," and the attacks are generally discontinued.

I will never forget the time when I finally managed to block a surprise attack from Sandweiss Sensei. I had been training for several years, and had always failed to block his surprise attacks. Whenever I was anticipating an attack and ready to respond, Sandweiss Sensei did not attack. He would always attack when I least expected it.

I certainly was not expecting a surprise attack on the day I finally passed this test. After attending a karate class with Scott Sensei at the Asian Martial Arts Studio, I was hurrying down a hallway at the University of Michigan Recreation Building to attend a karate class with Sandweiss Sensei. I had my gym bag in one hand, and I was almost late for class.

I saw Sandweiss Sensei coming down the hallway with a number of focus mitts in his arms. A focus mitt looks like a catcher's mitt with one side completely flat. It is used to practice hitting an object to develop more powerful punches, kicks, and strikes. It also protects the holder's hands from injury. Although the focus mitts had been ordered early in the semester, we had been waiting for them to arrive for a long time. I was excited to see that they had finally arrived.

I moved to the other side of the hallway to talk with him and get a closer look at the focus mitts. Just as I came to within a few feet of his body and was starting to comment on the focus mitts, Sandweiss Sensei stepped forward and thrust one of the focus mitts toward my face. Surprisingly, I had (and still have) no conscious recollection of seeing his attack coming toward my face. The next thing I knew I was looking up and saw that I had executed a perfect upper block with my one free arm. Without saying a word, Sandweiss Sensei took a few steps backward and we bowed to each other. We both knew that it was body knowledge that had enabled me to successfully block the attack.

This was the last time that Sandweiss Sensei ever did a surprise attack. Even though it happened over ten years ago, I can still remember it as clearly as though it happened only a few minutes ago.

The practitioner of karate also finds that the body knowledge developed from karate training manifests itself in other areas of life. For example, after making a diving catch playing baseball, I began to find myself executing forward rolls instead of just crashing to the ground. (A forward roll is an Aikido technique used to dissipate the impact of hitting the ground when falling forward. It is similar to a somersault, but the roll is done diagonally across the back and starts on the outside edge of the arm near the little finger.)

One of my training contemporaries in Ann Arbor was working at a computer when the shelf above him suddenly gave way. To the amazement of everyone else in the room, he instinctively executed an upper block. The block deflected the shelf (and its contents) over his body and saved him from harm.

Another karate student was walking in a crosswalk at the Detroit airport when a speeding car suddenly slammed on its brakes. When he saw that the car was about to hit him, he leaped into the air, did a modified Forward Roll across the hood of the car and landed on his feet in a perfect fighting stance. He was not harmed at all. Bystanders estimated that the car was moving at 35-45 miles per hour when he rolled across its hood.

These are just a few examples of how the body knowledge developed from karate training is applied in other areas of life besides fighting. Body knowledge is not something, however, that is easily acquired. The techniques and exercises must be practiced over and over again. Quality repetitions are the only way to become proficient in Karate-do. With this repeated practice, the body itself learns and internalizes the techniques and principles. This is a slow and gradual process. There are no short cuts or easy ways, but the rewards of such dedicated practice are both martially effective and personally fulfilling.

In my own personal training, I continue to strive to refine and perfect my execution and internalization of the techniques and principles of karate. This is the lifelong journey of self-discovery and self-development taken by serious practitioners of karate. I am confident that this book will aid you in your own personal journey.

MY TEACHERS OF SHOBAYASHI SHORIN RYU AND SHUDOKAN KARATE-DO

I began my training under Y. Jay Sandweiss Sensei in January of 1979. Sandweiss Sensei was the Head Instructor of the University of Michigan Shorin Ryu Karate-Do Club. He is one of the senior students of Karl W. Scott III Sensei, the Director of Training at the Asian Martial Arts Studio in Ann Arbor, Michigan. In 1980, I began training under Scott Sensei at the Asian Martial Arts Studio in addition to continuing my training under Sandweiss Sensei (See Photo 1).

Scott Sensei's first teacher was Herbert Z. Wong Sensei. Wong Sensei was the founder of the University of Michigan Shorin Ryu Karate-do and Hung-Gar Kung Fu Club in 1970. Wong Sensei was trained in both the Shudokan and Shobayashi Shorin Ryu systems of Karate-do, Sil-Lum Hung-Gar (Tiger-Crane) Kung Fu, Wing Chun Kung Fu, and a number of internal Chinese martial arts. Scott Sensei and Wong Sensei were responsible for combining the techniques and exercises of the Shudokan and Shorin Ryu systems of Karate-do into the materials set forth in this book.

Wong Sensei learned Shudokan Karate-do from his first Karate-do teacher, Walter E. Todd Sensei. Todd Sensei can be considered one of the first Renaissance men of the martial arts because of his extensive cross-training in different martial arts. Todd Sensei trained under a number of 10th dans in Judo, Karate-do and Aikido. Photo 2 (next page) was taken at the Asian Martial Arts Studio in April of 1994 during the 20th Anniversary celebration and shows my teachers and me.

I feel fortunate to be a student of Sandweiss Sensei and Scott Sensei and to have had the opportunity to train with Wong Sensei and Todd Sensei. These men are exceptional martial artists and inspirational teachers. They have freely shared their martial arts with me and have guided my development in the

Photo 1 — Scott, Moeller and Sandweiss (l-r)

martial arts. I have been influenced by all of these teachers, and each has contributed to my development in his own unique way. I am grateful for all they have taught me and am honored to have been one of their students. In my own training and teaching, I strive to follow the examples they have set.

Although I have never lived in the same city as Todd Sensei or Wong Sensei, I was fortunate to have been training at a time when they made multiple visits to the Asian Martial Arts Studio each year. This enabled me to take private lessons with them in addition to attending the classes and special seminars they taught. On several occasions, I have also trained at Todd Sensei's school in Oakland, California.

Although I left Ann Arbor in 1983, I return as often as possible to train with Scott Sensei and Sandweiss Sensei to continue my martial arts development. Even after sixteen years of training, I am still impressed by their martial skills and ability to impart their knowledge. Their dedication, perseverance and diligence in training is inspirational.

In the pages that follow, I have provided brief biographical sketches and stories from the lives of these modern-day masters of the martial arts. I hope you will find their lives and accomplishments as impressive and inspirational as I do. Chart 1 and Chart 2 on the following pages show where my teachers and I fit into the Shorin Ryu and Goju Ryu Karate-do lineages.

Photo 2 — Scott, Wong, Moeller, Todd and Sandweiss (l-r)

Chart 1

Shorin-Ryu Karate-do Lineage Chart
Sakugawa Line

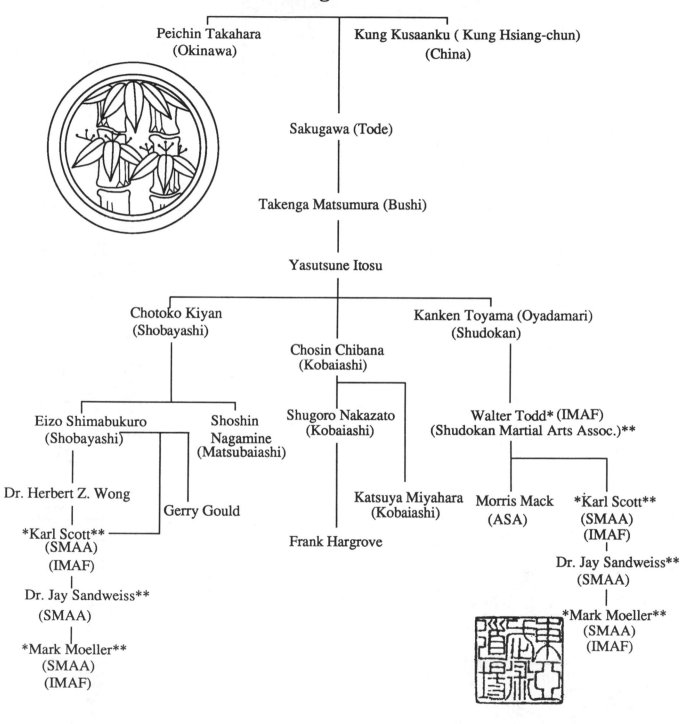

Peichin Takahara
(Okinawa)

Kung Kusaanku (Kung Hsiang-chun)
(China)

Sakugawa (Tode)

Takenga Matsumura (Bushi)

Yasutsune Itosu

Chotoko Kiyan
(Shobayashi)

Kanken Toyama (Oyadamari)
(Shudokan)

Chosin Chibana
(Kobaiashi)

Eizo Shimabukuro
(Shobayashi)

Shoshin
Nagamine
(Matsubaiashi)

Shugoro Nakazato
(Kobaiashi)

Walter Todd* (IMAF)
(Shudokan Martial Arts Assoc.)**

Dr. Herbert Z. Wong

Gerry Gould

Katsuya Miyahara
(Kobaiashi)

Morris Mack
(ASA)

*Karl Scott**
(SMAA)
(IMAF)

*Karl Scott**
(SMAA)
(IMAF)

Frank Hargrove

Dr. Jay Sandweiss**
(SMAA)

Dr. Jay Sandweiss**
(SMAA)

*Mark Moeller**
(SMAA)
(IMAF)

*Mark Moeller**
(SMAA)
(IMAF)

*IMAF Members (Kokusai Budoin, International Martial Arts Federation)
**SMAA Members (Shudokan Martial Arts Association)

Goju Ryu (Naha-te, Shorei Ryu) Lineage Chart
Higashionna Line

Arakaki

Doruko

Liu Liu Ko (China)

Kanryo Higashionna

Chojun Miyagi
(Goju Ryu)

Kanken Toyama
(Shudokan)

Kenwa Mabuni
(Shito Ryu)

Tatsuo Shimabukuro
(Isshin Ryu)

Kichiro Shimabukuro
(Isshin Ryu)

Seikichi Toguchi
(Okinawa)

Anthony Mirakian

Eizo Shimabukuro
(Shobayashi Shorin Ryu)

Arashira
(Okinawa)

Dr. Herbert Z. Wong

*Gogen Yamaguchi
(Japan) (Goju Kai)

*Eichi Miyazato
(Okinawa)

**Karl Scott*
(SMAA)
(IMAF)

Gosei Yamaguchi
(Goju Kai)

**Dr. Jay Sandweiss (SMAA)

**Mark Moeller*
(IMAF) (SMAA)

Ichikawa
(Doshinkan)

Morris Mack
(ASA)

**Walter Todd *
(Shudokan Martial Arts Assoc.)

Kanei Mabuni
(Shito Ryu)

Eizo Onisi
(Koeikan)

*Dr. Jay Sandweiss
(SMAA)

**Karl Scott*
(SMAA) (IMAF)

**Mark Moeller*
(IMAF)
(SMAA)

*IMAF Members (Kokusai Budoin, International Martial Arts Federation)
**SMAA Members (Shudokan Martial Arts Association)

Chart 2

WALTER E. TODD SENSEI (b. 1927)

In 1946, Walter E. Todd Sensei (Photo 3), while serving in the United States Army, began his martial arts training in Judo at the Kodokan in Tokyo, Japan. He was awarded his 1st dan in Kodokan Judo after a year of training as many as four hours a day. Shortly thereafter, he was accepted as a personal student of Kyuzo Mifune Sensei. Mifune Sensei was a 10th dan who is regarded as the finest Judo technician ever produced by the Kodokan. He was awarded the title *Meijin* ("Grandmaster") by Kokusai Budoin — International Martial Arts Federation. (This title originated prior to the modern-day black belt levels to indicate a person's level of skill and is similar to the samurai titles awarded in Japan during feudal times. This is the highest title given by Kokusai Budoin.) Todd Sensei continued his training in Judo until his tour of duty in the service ended.

He returned to his home and began teaching Judo at a community college in Oakland, California. One night a friend asked if he had seen the advertisement in the previous week's newspaper seeking individuals to work in Japan. After finding the advertisement, Todd Sensei immediately went to inquire about the job.

The woman who interviewed Todd Sensei told him that all the positions were already filled, but she then asked him to explain why he wanted to go to Japan. He told her that he wanted to resume his study of Judo and that he could train in the mornings, afternoons, or evenings to accommodate any work schedule. The woman was impressed with his answers and told him that most of the other individuals wanted to go to Japan primarily to see old girlfriends. She told him that she would speak to her superiors about him because she felt his motives for wanting to go to Japan were higher than the other candidates. She called a few days later to tell him that they had decided to take him instead of one of the others they had already hired. Todd Sensei left for Japan in 1947 and worked for the next two years in the Tokyo PX.

Upon his return to Japan, Todd Sensei resumed his training with Mifune Sensei at the Kodokan. He also sought out instruction in karate because he had read about it in a magazine back in the United States. A friend who knew of his interest took him to the Wado-Ryu Karate-do club that met at Meiji University, and he started training at the club. After a few months, he was invited to the Kyobashi police station in Tokyo where Grandmaster Hironishi Otsuka himself taught the classes three nights a week. Grandmaster Otsuka was the founder of the Wado-Ryu Karate-do system and had also been awarded the title of *Meijin* by Kokusai Budoin. In 1948, Todd Sensei became the first non-Japanese to study under Grandmaster Otsuka.

For the next two years, Todd Sensei spent most of his free time studying and practicing martial arts. He would go to Judo classes three nights a week and karate classes three other nights of the week. After class, he would generally go up to the roof of the building where he lived for additional training. He would practice what he had just learned in class over and over again until he was sure he could remember the basic pattern and key checkpoints. In this manner, he was able to learn a considerable amount in a short period of time. When the job at the Tokyo PX ended in 1950, Todd Sensei returned to the Oakland area.

Photo 3 — Todd Sensei

During most of the 1950s, Todd Sensei taught martial arts for the United States government. He worked as a civilian expert for the United States Air Force Strategic Air Command. He was an instructor in the Combat Measures Program at Travis Air Force Base in California from 1950-1956 and also taught at the United States Air Force Academy in Denver, Colorado. He was responsible for establishing the curriculum of the hand-to-hand combat program at the Academy. After establishing the initial program, Todd Sensei would frequently travel from California to Denver (often staying for several months at a time) to train both the instructors and the cadets.

It was through his martial arts instruction for the United States Air Force that Todd Sensei began studying Shotokan Karate-do with Isao Obata Sensei in 1951. (He also trained in Shotokan with Nishiyama Sensei and Kumata Sensei.) Obata Sensei was a senior student of Shotokan's founder, Gichin Funakoshi, and at that time the President of the Shotokan karate organization in Japan. Upon Obata Sensei's recommendation, Grandmaster Funakoshi approved Todd Sensei's promotion to 1st dan in Shotokan in 1953. Todd Sensei is believed to be the first non-Japanese black belt approved by Grandmaster Funakoshi.

At the end of 1958, Todd Sensei left the employment of the United States Air Force and opened a full-time, professional martial arts school in Oakland, California. The school was called the International Judo School. Over the years, Todd Sensei's Judo students have done very well in Judo competitions. (One of his students, George Harris, was the national Judo heavyweight champion for the United States in 1957, 1958, 1960, and 1961. Harris won a gold medal in the Pan American Games and came close to winning a medal in the 1964 Olympics.) The name of Todd Sensei's school was later changed to the International Judo, Karate and Aikido School as regular classes were offered in different arts. The school is one of the oldest in the country.

Todd Sensei's proficiency in Judo has been recognized by many organizations over the years. He received his 5th dan in Kodokan Judo in 1968, his 6th dan from the United States Judo Association in 1983, and his 8th dan from Kokusai

Budoin in 1993. He is currently the only person in North America to have received an 8th dan from Kokusai Budoin. Kokusai Budoin also gave him the title of *Kyoshi* ("Full Professor" or "Master") of Judo in 1989. *Kyoshi* is the highest title that has been awarded to anyone in North America by Kokusai Budoin.

In 1958, Todd Sensei met Yoko Takahashi Sensei. Takahashi Sensei was a 5th dan in Grandmaster Kanken Toyama's Shudokan Karate-do system and an advanced student at the Aikido Hombu Dojo ("Headquarters School") in Japan. He had also studied a number of other Japanese martial arts including Judo, Iaido, and Kendo. Takahashi Sensei was living in the United States to study American farming techniques by working as a laborer on a farm in Los Angeles, California. One of Todd Sensei's students had met Takahashi Sensei at a social function in Los Angeles and later told Todd Sensei about Takahashi Sensei's martial arts background. Todd Sensei was very interested in meeting Takahashi Sensei to see if he could learn more karate so he asked the student to try and find him the next time he was in Los Angeles. He also asked the student to invite Takahashi Sensei to visit the school in Oakland. Some time later, the student again met him, and, after describing Todd Sensei's school and martial arts background, gave him Todd Sensei's name and address.

Todd Sensei was very surprised when Takahashi Sensei arrived at his home unannounced one night and introduced himself. (It turns out that Takahashi Sensei was interested in finding someone with whom he could practice Aikido. Because of Todd Sensei's extensive background in Judo, Takahashi Sensei knew that he would be sufficiently skilled at *ukemi* [falling techniques] to be able to take the Aikido falls without injury.) After visiting for a while and describing his martial arts background and experience, Takahashi Sensei offered to teach Todd Sensei karate if he would be his partner for Aikido practice. Todd Sensei readily agreed, and it was at this point that he began learning Shudokan Karate-do. Training with Takahashi Sensei turned out to be a double benefit for Todd Sensei because he learned Aikido as well as Karate-do from a highly qualified teacher.

For the next three years, Takahashi Sensei traveled from Los Angeles to Oakland almost every weekend and whenever he had time off from work to teach karate and practice Aikido with Todd Sensei. In order to make this easier for him, Todd Sensei bought him a car after a few months. During these visits, Takahashi Sensei would stay at Todd Sensei's house.

Takahashi Sensei was a very dedicated martial artist. After several months of visits, Todd Sensei woke up at 2:00 a.m. one night and noticed that Takahashi Sensei had quietly slipped out of the house and was practicing martial arts in the backyard. He continued to practice for over an hour. The next morning, Takahashi Sensei got up early as though he had slept through the entire night. Whenever Todd Sensei awoke during the middle of the night, he would almost always find Takahashi Sensei practicing outside. Todd Sensei never spoke about these late-night workouts with Takahashi Sensei, but he was very impressed. These workouts show how dedicated Takahashi Sensei was to practicing and perfecting his martial arts.

Because of his previous karate and martial arts experience, Todd Sensei made rapid progress. The International Judo, Karate and Aikido School became the first dojo (martial arts school) in the San Francisco/Oakland Bay area to offer regular Karate-do classes. Todd Sensei was also one of the first people in the United States to teach Karate-do.

Upon the recommendation of Takahashi Sensei, Grandmaster Toyama appointed Todd Sensei *Shibucho* (or Director) of Shudokan Karate-do for the United States in 1959. As Shibucho, Todd Sensei was put in charge of Shudokan Karate-do in the United States. In 1961, Grandmaster Toyama promoted Todd Sensei to the rank of 4th dan.

When Grandmaster Toyama died in 1966 and left no successor, Todd Sensei automatically became solely in charge of the United States. As *Shibucho*, he has the authority to award any rank in Shudokan Karate-do in the United States. Of course, he cannot promote himself and therefore must have been pleased when his promotion to 8th dan was approved in 1978 by Hatoyama, the son of Grandmaster Toyama.

In addition to teaching him karate, Takahashi Sensei was also responsible for Todd Sensei's Aikido training. (Todd Sensei had done some Aikido training with Kenji Tomiki Sensei, a Judo and Aikido Master he had met in Japan in 1948 and 1949, but it was Takahashi Sensei who became his primary Aikido teacher.) At first, Todd Sensei was not interested in learning Aikido because it did not seem very effective. He felt he could have easily prevented Takahashi Sensei from throwing him. Out of respect and politeness, however, he allowed himself to be thrown. As their relationship developed and after they had spent time working together on the mat, Takahashi Sensei suggested that Todd Sensei try to counter his techniques whenever he thought he could do so effectively. Gradually, Todd Sensei started trying to do this during their training sessions. He was very surprised to find that regardless of how hard he tried to execute a counter, Takahashi Sensei, who was a much smaller man, still managed to throw him easily.

This caused Todd Sensei to reassess his opinion of Aikido and he began to pay closer attention to the techniques that Takahashi Sensei was using. With his own students, Todd Sensei began to work on applying these techniques himself. After a while, he asked Takahashi Sensei to critique his execution of these techniques. When Takahashi Sensei saw that he was interested in learning Aikido as well as Karate-do, he began to spend part of their training time instructing him in Aikido. When Todd Sensei became relatively proficient in Aikido (and at Takahashi Sensei's encouragement), Aikido classes were added to the Judo and Karate-do classes taught at the school. It was at this point that the school was renamed to the International Judo, Karate and Aikido School.

In addition to teaching him Aikido directly, Takahashi Sensei also introduced and arranged for Todd Sensei to train with Koichi Tohei Sensei, then Chief Instructor at the Aikido Hombu Dojo ("Headquarters School") in Japan. When Tohei Sensei would travel through the United States, he would often stay at Todd Sensei's house while teaching seminars and classes at Todd Sensei's school and other dojos in the San Francisco Bay area.

Todd Sensei's promotions in Aikido were recommended by Takahashi Sensei. Todd Sensei's 1st and 2nd dan certificates were signed by the founder of Aikido, Grandmaster Morihei Ueshiba, himself. These certificates were personally delivered by Tohei Sensei. He received his 2nd dan in 1965.

Todd Sensei decided shortly after getting this promotion that he did not want to be formally involved with another martial arts organization and would simply practice and teach Aikido for the sake of the art itself. (In order to see that his students received proper recognition and black belt promotions in Aikido, however, Todd Sensei would recommend promotions to Tohei Sensei for his approval. Tohei Sensei has never failed to approve a recommendation made by Todd Sensei.) In 1994, Kokusai Budoin awarded Todd Sensei the rank of 6th dan in recognition of his knowledge and understanding of Aikido. Kokusai Budoin also gave him the title of *Renshi* ("Assistant Professor" or "Expert") in Aikido.

One of the most impressive things about Todd Sensei is that although he has always taught Judo, Karate, and Aikido separately, as distinct martial arts, and in accordance with their traditional emphases, he has been able to integrate all these arts within himself. This integration is demonstrated by his ability to flow from one martial art to another in free-style sparring. He simply uses the most effective technique for the situation and is not bound or limited by the constraints of any particular martial art. This is done in an effortless manner with a minimum of conscious thought. His body intuitively executes the most appropriate technique.

His diverse martial arts background has also enabled him to identify and utilize techniques from one art that are often hidden in another art. For example, his extensive experience in Judo and Aikido has enabled him to discover the hidden grappling, joint-locking, and throwing techniques that are found in many traditional karate *kata*. His Karate-do training insures that Judo and Aikido defenses against striking attacks would be effective against someone trained in a martial art that specializes in punching and kicking.

One of the toughest, if not the toughest, challenges of Todd Sensei's life came in 1980. He was involved in a head-on car accident which occurred when the driver of the other car fell asleep and crossed into his lane. The three occupants of the other car were all killed. Todd Sensei's feet went through the floorboards of the car and the steering wheel broke off because he had pushed his arms into an unbendable arm position from the martial arts immediately before impact. His right heel was crushed, both his knees were broken, and his left femur bone was broken. At first, the doctors thought they might have to amputate his right foot, but they managed to save it. They told him, however, that he would probably never be able to walk again, let alone do martial arts, because of his broken knees. He was in the hospital for four months.

The accident forced Todd Sensei to draw on everything he had learned in the martial arts and reach deep inside himself to find the inner strength and resources to recover from his injuries. It would have been much easier for him to give up and resign himself to life in a wheelchair. But Todd Sensei has never been a quitter.

He recalls thinking about one of the guiding principles of his life that he had frequently relayed to his students: If you really want something, you have to be willing to fight and sacrifice enough to accomplish it. He also used his students as a motivational force. He did not want to be a hypocrite — either in their eyes or in his own eyes. He decided that regardless of the physical pain or embarrassment of falling down, he would try to take a few steps as soon as the doctors said it would be safe to try. If he was not successful, he would try again and again. Even if he never managed to walk again, he and his students would know that he had tried as hard as he could and had never given up.

It was not easy at first. His legs were badly damaged and he was already 54 years old. Nevertheless, he persisted. Within six months of his release from the hospital, he was able to walk using only crutches. Within a year, he was able to discard the crutches. He also resumed his full-time teaching and training schedule. Although there are still some techniques that he cannot do as effectively as he could before the accident, he continues to work on improving them.

Even when he was confined to a wheelchair, Todd Sensei was still able to effectively use his martial arts skills. One day when he was at his dojo in the wheelchair, a black belt he knew from another school came to visit him. In the course of a conversation about various techniques, the man stated that it was impossible to escape from a rear double-hand grab without using a kicking technique. This remark must have hurt Todd Sensei because he was facing the possibility that he might never walk again, let alone be able to do any kicking techniques. Todd Sensei, however, did not get upset. Rather, he maintained the calm demeanor of a true warrior and said he would like to see if the statement was true. He asked the man to stand behind his wheelchair and grasp both his wrists as tightly as possible. After confirming that the man was ready to resist his efforts to escape, he proceeded to easily throw the man into a heap on the concrete. He then asked the man if he would like to try again, but the man quickly declined.

One of the unexpected benefits of the accident was that it helped make him even more effective as a teacher. Todd Sensei was, and is, a virtual genius when it comes to the ability to isolate and understand martial arts principles. Because he was confined to a wheelchair and on crutches for over a year, he could not use his body to demonstrate principles and more effective ways to execute techniques. Instead, he had to rely solely on his ability to articulate these comments and suggestions in words. As a result, he has become even more adept at explaining key ideas and concepts in the martial arts. Because he can now demonstrate as well as explain principles and techniques more effectively, it has made it even easier for his students to understand and apply his teachings.

In the early 1980s, Todd Sensei formed the American Shudokan Association to promote the development and preservation of traditional martial arts. In 1994, the name was changed to the Shudokan Martial Arts Association. There

were originally only three divisions, but as highly qualified martial artists (with strong backgrounds in other traditional styles) joined the Association, new divisions were formed under their leadership. The head of each division is a person who has had substantial training in a traditional martial art and has demonstrated a thorough knowledge and understanding of, and proficiency in, his or her particular art. All promotions must be approved by the head of the particular division to ensure that high and consistent standards are maintained. The Shudokan Martial Arts Association currently has separate divisions and offers rank in Traditional Karate-do, Aikido, Judo, Traditional Jujutsu, Iaido, and Goshin-Jutsu.

In addition to overseeing the operations of the Shudokan Martial Arts Association, Todd Sensei continues to practice and refine his own martial arts skills. In 1993, he relocated the International Judo, Karate and Aikido School to Berkeley, California. At the time of the move, the name was changed to the International Martial Arts School. Todd Sensei also continues to share his knowledge by teaching at his school and at the schools of his students across the United States.

The following quotes from Todd Sensei summarize his philosophy of the martial arts:

A Teacher who has mastered his medium has evolved a philosophy from such an experience and whether we agree or not, his thoughts act like a catalyst on our own. In this way, he has contributed to the dynamic ideas of our time. Rarely do such concepts get written down clearly so students all over the world may read that which is their ultimate expression.

It is not the mere technique that is important. Rather, technique is a vital medium of expression, a way to get in touch with the most vibrant elements of existence. It represents a way of life, a way of working, a process which leads one to discover ways to fulfill oneself and to make a special resonance available to others.

One of the things I have always admired about Todd Sensei is his openness to new ideas. For example, when he sees students executing a technique in a manner that is unusual or different from the standard way, he does not immediately criticize and attempt to change them. Instead, he asks the students to explain what they are doing and how they envision they would apply the technique in an actual encounter. If the interpretation/application is realistic and effective, Todd Sensei allows them to continue executing the technique in that manner and may offer suggestions on how to make that application more effective. He may also change his own execution and explanation of the technique if the new interpretation is exceptionally good. If the student does not have a particular application/interpretation in mind or if it is ineffective, Todd Sensei will then correct their execution of the technique.

By adopting this approach, Todd Sensei encourages his students to explore different options and increase their understanding of the martial arts. They are also encouraged to express their own individual uniqueness and personality through the medium of their martial arts. Todd Sensei's attitude and philosophy also ensure that the martial arts do not remain static. Instead, they are continually being developed and improved. By encouraging this creativity and experimentation, Todd Sensei's students become innovators and independent thinkers.

In addition, Todd Sensei also continues to expand his own knowledge and understanding of the martial arts. Despite his almost 50 years of training (and almost 45 years as a full-time martial arts instructor), Todd Sensei will be the first to tell you that he is continually learning new things from his beginning and advanced students. He believes there is always something new to learn in the martial arts, and that one must be open and willing to learn from one's teachers, peers, and students. He is not concerned with trying to impress others with how much he knows. Rather, his concern is solely with developing the art, his students, and his own knowledge and understanding.

In this way, he both lives and epitomizes the samurai maxim of eliminating one's ego and concern for the self in both martial and non-martial situations. By doing this, the samurai were able to achieve things that would not be possible if they were limited by the bounds of self-interest. In combat, they could allow themselves to react intuitively (and thereby more effectively) because they were not worrying about saving their own lives. For Todd Sensei, this attitude and approach has allowed him to learn many things that he may never have discovered without this open mind and ability to control his ego.

Photo 4 — Scott, Moeller, Todd and Sandweiss (l-r)

HERBERT Z. WONG SENSEI

Herbert Z. Wong Sensei's (Photo 5) first exposure to the martial arts occurred in the Chinese schools he attended as a young boy in San Francisco's Chinatown. Martial arts were taught as part of the cultural arts curriculum and informally at Chinese community centers. In 1959, Wong Sensei began his formal martial arts training in Shudokan Karate-do with Walter E. Todd Sensei at the International Judo, Karate and Aikido School. He was one of the first group of students at the school to earn a black belt in karate, which he received in 1961. He continued to train diligently and was awarded his 2nd dan in 1963.

The United States Army drafted Wong Sensei in 1963 and sent him to Okinawa. After arriving in Okinawa, Wong Sensei visited many karate schools while waiting for a letter of introduction from Grandmaster Kanken Toyama that was being sent to Todd Sensei. Because of the delays of international mail, the letter did not arrive for over six months.

During that time, he began training with Grandmaster Eizo Shimabukuro in Shobayashi Shorin Ryu Karate-do. This decision was based on two factors: Grandmaster Shimabukuro's martial proficiency and his 10th dan certificate. Wong Sensei recognized the signature and seal of Grandmaster Toyama on the certificate. This led him to believe that he would be training in a school with a consistent Karate-do lineage.

Out of respect for Grandmaster Shimabukuro and to show that he had a proper attitude, Wong Sensei did not even attempt to wear the black belt he had received from Todd Sensei. Instead, he put on a white belt and began as a beginner. It seems likely that this action would have been viewed very favorably by Grandmaster Shimabukuro and would have earned Wong Sensei a fair amount of respect. Grandmaster Shimabukuro certainly would have seen that he had a substantial karate background, and yet Wong Sensei demonstrated that he was willing to "empty his cup" and accept the teachings of Grandmaster Shimabukuro.

When the letter of introduction finally arrived, Wong Sensei realized that he was not in the school that Grandmaster Toyama had intended for him. Wong Sensei realized that it would be both disrespectful and foolish to stop training with Grandmaster Shimabukuro. The Shorin Ryu he was learning emphasized power sources and techniques that were different from the Shudokan he had previously studied. He also recognized that it was a unique opportunity to train with an exceptional karate master and to broaden his knowledge of karate.

In addition to his good fortune in finding Grandmaster Shimabukuro, Wong Sensei was also fortunate to have received an Army assignment that did not require him to work irregular hours or weekends. He took full advantage of this schedule and devoted himself to the study and practice of karate. Wong Sensei attended classes and trained with Grandmaster Shimabukuro for 2-3 hours each night during the week and 4-5 hours on Saturdays and Sundays.

Throughout the time he was in Okinawa, Wong Sensei managed to train almost every single day. Because of this dedication and his previous experience, Wong Sensei earned his black belt in

Photo 5 — Wong Sensei

Shobayashi Shorin Ryu near the end of 1964. He was awarded his 2nd dan in August of 1965, which was shortly before he finished his military service and returned to the United States.

Before returning to the United States, however, Wong Sensei had an opportunity to visit Grandmaster Toyama in Japan. During the course of their visit, Grandmaster Toyama asked him to demonstrate some of the *kata* he had learned from Grandmaster Shimabukuro. When he had finished, Grandmaster Toyama complemented him on his demonstration and said it was good to see that traditional Okinawan Karate-do was being preserved by Grandmaster Shimabukuro.

After returning from Okinawa, Wong Sensei resumed his undergraduate studies at San Francisco State University and continued to practice Shobayashi Shorin Ryu. In 1965, he started the Asian Martial Arts School in San Francisco with Andrew Chan Sensei. He also began training in Sil-Lum Hung Gar (Tiger-Crane) Kung Fu under *Sifu* Y.C. Wong in San Francisco that same year. (*Sifu* is another name for teacher.) Wong Sensei was one of Master Wong's first three students in the United States. Wong Sensei continued to train with Master Wong and teach at the Asian Martial Arts School until he left the San Francisco Bay area to pursue his graduate studies.

In September of 1970, Wong Sensei started in the doctoral program at The University of Michigan in Ann Arbor. While simultaneously pursuing his doctorate degree in clinical and organizational psychology, he was also teaching classes in Okinawan Karate-do and Chinese Kung Fu. In the beginning, Wong Sensei accepted only four students, including Karl W. Scott III Sensei and Gary Hu Sensei. All four of these individuals already had previous martial arts experience. With the exception of two-person work, the majority of class time was spent in individualized instruction. (The length of the classes varied because it would depend on whether they were forced to leave the Michigan Recreation Building at closing time or were allowed to let themselves out after the building was locked up.) Wong Sensei taught both Okinawan Karate-do and Chinese Kung Fu, but would always make a clear distinction as to which art he was teaching at the time. Discipline was strict and repetitions of the basics were emphasized.

It was a few years before Wong Sensei accepted any other students. This occurred when Wong Sensei felt that his original students were ready to assist with the teaching of larger classes. At that point, he formed a university club known as the Okinawan Shorin Ryu and Chinese Kung Fu Group. (The name of the club was later changed to the University of Michigan Shorin Ryu Karate-do Club, and it still continues to meet several times a week.) Because of his karate skills and reputation as a weapons expert, Wong Sensei's classes were very well attended once opened to the general public. Most of the students had considerable experience in other styles of karate and other martial arts. (Mark Zaremba Sensei, currently a 5th dan and one of the senior karate instructors at the Asian Martial Arts Studio, began his training shortly after the club was formed.) The group class would last for about an hour, and then Wong Sensei would spend the next 3-4 hours working individually with the assistant instructors.

After almost four years, Wong Sensei tested his assistant instructors and promoted them to black belt. Shortly after these promotions, he strongly suggested that one of them, with the help of the others, should open a full-time martial arts school. In 1974, Hu Sensei and Scott Sensei opened a school in Ann Arbor. This school has continued to exist since that time and is now known as the Asian Martial Arts Studio. Scott Sensei has been the Director of Training at the school since 1979, and he continues to carry on Wong Sensei's karate legacy in Ann Arbor. In 1974, Wong Sensei was also made the head of Shorin Ryu for the Midwestern and Southern Divisions of the United States by Grandmaster Shimabukuro.

After receiving his doctorate degree, Wong Sensei returned to the San Francisco Bay area in 1975 to run a psychiatric clinic and psychology training center. A few years later he started doing consulting work in addition to running the clinic. He now has his own consulting firm that specializes in management consulting and organizational development.

Over the years, Wong Sensei and Andrew Chan Sensei also ran a number of martial arts schools together. Wong Sensei continues to make regular trips to Ann Arbor to teach seminars, classes, and private lessons at the Asian Martial Arts Studio.

In addition, he continues to travel to Okinawa to train with Grandmaster Shimabukuro. He has received a number of promotions over the years and was awarded his 7th dan in 1975. He was also awarded the title of *Shihan* ("Full Professor" or "Teaching Model") by Grandmaster Shimabukuro.

In 1993, Wong Sensei moved to Boston, Massachusetts where he continues to run his consulting business. Although he is not currently involved in a local karate school, he continues to travel to Ann Arbor to teach at the Asian Martial Arts Studio. I have also been fortunate to have had Wong Sensei teach at my school when he was in Atlanta for a psychology convention.

One of the things I have always admired about Wong Sensei is his ability to work with students at any level and to almost instantly assess what a student needs to learn at that particular point in his or her training. I can still remember my first private lesson with Wong Sensei. My friend and I had been training about six months and had just finished learning the required materials for our first promotion. Wong Sensei asked us what we wanted to work on during our lesson. On the recommendation of Sandweiss Sensei, we said whatever he felt we needed to work on.

He asked us to demonstrate Taikyuku Shodan kata (which is described in Chapter XII of Part II). As soon as we finished, he told us he knew exactly what we would do and said we would at least triple, and probably quadruple, our punching power by the end of the half hour lesson. Using sheets of paper as targets, he proceeded to show us how to use our legs, hips, and arms as one coordinated unit to increase the power and effectiveness of our punches. Based on the loudness and sharpness of the snap of the paper, we were able to assess the relative power of our punches. We were both very pleased (and somewhat amazed) to find that we easily more than tripled our punching power by the end of the lesson.

Throughout the years as I have had other private lessons with Wong Sensei, I have always found that he knew exactly what I needed to work on at that particular point in my training. Because of his teaching skills, I also noticed a significant improvement in my understanding and execution of the principles or techniques he covered in these lessons. My experiences with Wong Sensei during these lessons have not been unique. I have heard similar comments from many other students after they had completed a class or lesson with Wong Sensei.

Photo 6 — Scott, Sandweiss, Moeller and Wong (l-r)

KARL W. SCOTT III SENSEI (b. 1953)

Karl W. Scott III Sensei (Photo 7) began his martial arts training in Judo in 1965 in the eastern suburbs of Detroit, Michigan. Over the course of the next five years, he also studied Tae Kwon Do and Tang Soo Do, two Korean styles of karate. He progressed to the highest level of brown belt in Tae Kwon Do. Although he was asked to test for his black belt, he declined because he had already started training with Wong Sensei.

Scott Sensei first learned of Wong Sensei through a Chinese friend who had a Tae Kwon Do Club in Dearborn, Michigan. This friend knew Wong Sensei through a Chinese student association. At the time, Scott Sensei was very interested in learning Okinawan karate weapons and had learned that Wong Sensei was an expert. In the summer of 1970, the friend arranged for Wong Sensei to observe Scott Sensei teach one of the Dearborn Club's children's classes (which Scott Sensei was teaching for him that summer). Wong Sensei must have been sufficiently impressed with Scott Sensei because after the class was over Wong Sensei invited him to be his third (and at that point in time, final) karate student. It is interesting that all three of these original karate students had significant prior experience in Korean styles of karate. This is probably due to the fact that at this time there were very few karate schools in the southeastern portion of Michigan that were not teaching Korean karate.

Wong Sensei proved to be a demanding teacher. The group met three times a week and each class lasted 4-5 hours. In addition to the three classes a week, Wong Sensei would also frequently work with Scott Sensei privately on other days. With the exception of two-person training, Wong Sensei would spend almost all of the time working individually with the students.

In order to test Scott Sensei's attitude and perseverance as well as to thoroughly ingrain critical movements into Scott Sensei's mind and body, Wong Sensei required him to spend the first few months of training working only on circle-stepping in a front stance and other basic exercises. (Circle stepping is the method used for moving forward and backward in a front stance in Okinawan karate. It involves tracing a crescent-shaped arc along the ground with the ball of one foot to move the leg forward or backward into position before shifting the body weight into the next stance. This is done while maintaining one's balance on the other leg which is bent as much as possible to stay close to the ground for maximum stability and balance. Circle stepping is described in the section on *Kiyan* Lines in Chapter IX of Part II.) In addition to being very taxing on his leg muscles, Scott Sensei quickly developed blisters on his feet because all training was done on hardwood floors without shoes. There were many times during these first months when these blisters broke and Scott Sensei would have to wash his feet with alcohol to prevent infection after training. At night, he would ice his feet to keep the swelling down.

Despite the limited material to practice and the physical discomforts, Scott Sensei never complained and continued to work to the best of his ability on whatever Wong Sensei told him to do. After this initial "testing" period was over, Wong Sensei did not begin to teach the weapons that had initially attracted Scott Sensei. (In fact,

Photo 7 — Scott Sensei

it would be almost three years before Scott Sensei began to work with any of the Okinawan weapons.) Instead, Wong Sensei began to systematically work on Scott Sensei's execution of other basic techniques. It seems that Wong Sensei wanted to instill in Scott Sensei an understanding of the importance of the basics as well as to correct his execution of these fundamental techniques.

When Wong Sensei was satisfied with Scott Sensei's basics, Wong Sensei began to teach him the drills, *kata*, and two-person exercises of the Shobayashi Shorin Ryu system from white belt to black belt. When Scott Sensei and the others had reached the level of proficiency where Wong Sensei felt they could help instruct, a university club was formed and the general public was permitted to join the classes. This club was known as the Okinawan Shorin Ryu and Chinese Kung Fu Group.

After almost four years of intensive training, Scott Sensei was asked to formally test for his black belt in Shobayashi Shorin Ryu. He was given only one week's notice to prepare. The test lasted three hours (without breaks) and Scott Sensei was awarded his black belt in February of 1974. (Mark Zaremba Sensei also participated in the test and was awarded his brown belt.)

Scott Sensei was a model student. This was especially true in the key areas of attitude, heart, discipline, and spirit. He was almost always the first one to arrive and the last one to leave classes. He also practiced his basics every day outside of the regular classes. Because of his dedication, Wong Sensei frequently cited Scott Sensei as an example for the other students. He was the only one of the three students who did not pay for lessons. Although he tried on many occasions to pay, Wong Sensei always refused. (Scott Sensei recalls that Wong Sensei would always tell him that he was paying for his lessons with the hard work and spirit he put into his training.)

Throughout the entire time that Wong Sensei was in Ann Arbor, Scott Sensei never complained about the materials Wong Sensei required him to practice. He also never missed a single class or private lesson. One of the things that makes this perfect attendance record even more remarkable

(and shows Scott Sensei's dedication and spirit) is that for four years Scott Sensei was living in an eastern suburb of Detroit. In order to train with Wong Sensei, he had to drive 55 miles each way to Ann Arbor. He continued to make this 110-mile round-trip commute until 1974.

He moved to Ann Arbor at that time to help Gary Hu Sensei start and run a full-time martial arts school. This school was known as K.E.I. until 1977, when the name was changed to the Asian Martial Arts Studio, its current name. Scott Sensei was the Assistant Head Instructor from the time the school opened until he left for Okinawa in 1978. (Upon his return from Okinawa, Hu Sensei made Scott Sensei the Acting Head Instructor and then the Head Instructor.)

Shortly after the school opened, Wong Sensei arranged for Todd Sensei, who at that time was the Chief Instructor for the United States for the Doshinkan organization, to visit the school with a delegation of karate masters who were touring the United States. (Doshinkan was the name chosen by Isao Ichikawa Sensei, a 10th dan and senior student of Grandmaster Toyama, for his Shudokan organization.) From that time on, the Asian Martial Arts Studio began paying for Todd Sensei to make regular visits to Ann Arbor and the school was officially affiliated with both the Shobayashi Shorin Ryu and Shudokan organizations.

It was at this point in time that Wong Sensei, Hu Sensei, and Scott Sensei formally incorporated *kata* and techniques from the Shudokan system into the progression of materials taught in the Karate-do Program. (Up until this time, the Shudokan materials were only taught to the more senior students.) Karate-do students at the Asian Martial Arts Studio then began receiving identical rank in Shobayashi Shorin Ryu and Shudokan Karate-do with every promotion. Despite the incorporation of these materials into the Karate-do Program, the Asian Martial Arts Studio has always kept both the Shobayashi Shorin Ryu and Shudokan styles distinct and consistent with their historical and stylistic emphases.

During his visits to Ann Arbor, Todd Sensei also began teaching Scott Sensei Aikido and Judo. Regular Aikido classes were started at the Asian

Martial Arts Studio in 1976. (Scott Sensei received his black belt in Aikido in 1979. Scott Sensei currently holds the rank of 6th dan in Aikido which he received from Todd Sensei in 1994. He earned his black belt in Judo in 1985.)

One of the specialties that Wong Sensei emphasized in Scott Sensei's training was inside fighting techniques. An important part of inside fighting is the ability to generate a tremendous amount of force over a very short distance. This is sometimes referred to as "short power" or the "one-inch punch." It requires both an extremely rapid contraction of muscles and an ability to utilize the body's internal energy (called *ki* in Japanese and *chi* in Chinese). The following story illustrates the success that Scott Sensei achieved in developing short power.

One day after completing his short power training drills, Scott Sensei was working with some of the senior students to help them prepare for their black belt test. One part of the test involves free-style sparring with armor. The armor is one of the training aids used in the Shobayshi Shorin Ryu system to develop punching power and a feeling for hitting an object. It also allows the wearer to experience a full force blow with a greatly reduced chance of injury. The armor is used to make sparring more like an actual fight. In Okinawa, the armor used is Kendo armor, which covers the torso of the body and is made of bamboo covered with a thin layer of material. At the Asian Martial Arts Studio, the armor looks the same as the Kendo armor used in Okinawa, but it has been specially designed for use in karate training by modern-day manufacturers. Instead of a bamboo core to withstand the impact and protect the wearer, the core is made of reinforced fiberglass that is advertised as unbreakable.

In the course of the sparring session, Scott Sensei moved his hand inside the other person's arms until it was 1-2 inches away from the armor. As he began to punch, he channeled all of his body's energy into his fist and imagined it penetrating through the armor. The fiberglass could not withstand the force and was cleanly broken. Everyone who was present was amazed. No one else at the Asian Martial Arts Studio had ever broken the armor — even after striking it with full-range punches and various kicks. Fortunately, the person wearing the armor was not seriously hurt and suffered only a few bruised ribs. After breaking several other sets of armor on different occasions, Scott Sensei stopped working with the armor to prevent injuries to the wearer and because of the cost of continually replacing the damaged sets. As of the writing of this book, there still is no one else who has ever broken the armor — let alone broken it with a one-inch punch.

In April of 1978, Scott Sensei left Ann Arbor with Zaremba Sensei to seek additional instruction from Todd Sensei and Grandmaster Shimabukuro. When he left, he did not know if he would ever return. After training for a month in Todd Sensei's school, Scott Sensei and Zaremba Sensei went to Okinawa for six weeks of intensive training with Grandmaster Shimabukuro.

They lived with Sandweiss Sensei and had extensive private and group lessons with Grandmaster Shimabukuro. Grandmaster Shimabukuro must have been impressed with their karate skills because Scott Sensei and Zaremba Sensei were invited to join Sandweiss Sensei on Grandmaster Shimabukuro's demonstration team. All three participated in a demo given at a local Marine Corps base. Shortly before leaving Okinawa, Scott Sensei received his 4th dan. (Scott Sensei had received his 2nd dan in 1975 and his 3rd dan in 1977 from Wong Sensei. He returned to Okinawa again in 1984 to train with Grandmaster Shimabukuro and was promoted to 5th dan at that time.)

After returning from Okinawa, Scott Sensei and Sandweiss Sensei stayed in Oakland and continued to train with Todd Sensei. Because of his family ties in Detroit, Scott Sensei returned to Ann Arbor near the end of the summer in 1978. Upon his return, Hu Sensei asked Scott Sensei to take over the Asian Martial Arts Studio because he was returning to graduate school. Although there were only a few students left in the school, Scott Sensei saw this as an opportunity to continue the tradition started by Wong Sensei and develop the school according to his own vision. He took over in March of 1979.

The Asian Martial Arts Studio has thrived under his leadership. It has grown from a handful of students to over 200 active students. Separate programs are taught with regular classes in Shobayashi Shorin Ryu and Shudokan Karate-do, Aikido, and both internal and external styles of Chinese Kung Fu, including Sil-Lum Hung-Gar, T'ai Chi Ch'uan, Bagua, and Hsing-Yi. In all these programs, the moral and philosophical aspects of the martial arts are stressed in addition to the physical techniques and fighting principles.

The Asian Martial Arts Studio has also become a center for the study and promotion of a greater awareness and appreciation of Asian culture. Scott Sensei was personally responsible for the introduction of instruction in traditional Chinese lion dancing at the Asian Martial Arts Studio. (Chinese lion dancing is traditionally an extension of Chinese martial arts and is practiced in many Kung Fu schools.)

One of Scott Sensei's visions for the Asian Martial Arts Studio was that it be more than just a place for individuals to learn martial arts. Instead, he has always seen it as a training center for instructors. As a result, the curriculum and classes emphasize a thorough understanding of the principles and techniques in addition to the ability to execute them properly. There is also a heavy emphasis on physical conditioning and calisthenics. Scott Sensei has always believed that instructors should not only know more than the students, but should also be in better physical condition. In every class, the instructors (including Scott Sensei) do all of the push-ups, sit-ups, and other calisthenics with the students. They are not allowed to simply call the count. In addition to maintaining their own physical condition, this also helps the instructors bond with the students because everyone in the class goes through the workout together. Instructors are also expected to continue their own training and conditioning outside of classes.

Scott Sensei has succeeded in creating a top-notch training center for instructors. Many of Scott Sensei's students, including Sandweiss Sensei and Zaremba Sensei to name only a few, have remained in Ann Arbor and become exceptional instructors at the Asian Martial Arts Studio. Others, including Nicklaus Suino Sensei and myself, have started their own schools. Suino Sensei currently teaches Shorin Ryu and Shudokan Karate-do, Iaido, Nihon Jujutsu, and Judo at his school, the Institute for Traditional Martial Arts in Lansing, Michigan. In 1994, he published his first book entitled *The Art of Japanese Swordsmanship — A Manual on Eishin Ryu Iaido*. Suino Sensei is currently working on a second book on Iaido.

In addition to developing his own school, Scott Sensei has also played an important role in a number of prestigious martial arts organization. He is the Division Director of the Traditional Karate-do Division of the Shudokan Martial Arts Association and oversees all division promotions. He is also currently the highest ranking member of its Aikido Division. The Asian Martial Arts Studio also serves as the Eastern United States Headquarters for the Shudokan Martial Arts Association. Scott Sensei currently holds the rank of 7th dan in Shudokan Karate-do (awarded in 1993) and 6th dan in Aikido (awarded in 1994).

In 1988, Scott Sensei became involved with Kokusai Budoin — International Martial Arts Federation. Kokusai Budoin is an association that was formed in 1952 to foster the promotion of friendship and cooperation among Budo (Japanese martial arts) practitioners and supporters. It is currently comprised of the following divisions: Karate-do, Judo, Aikido, Kendo, Iaido, Nihon Jujutsu, Batto Jutsu, Kobudo, Aikijujutsu, and Kyudo. The membership list includes many famous 10th dans and legendary practitioners of Japanese martial arts.

Scott Sensei's abilities were quickly recognized by Kokusai Budoin. He was awarded a 4th dan in the Karate-do Division at the time of his acceptance as a member of Kokusai Budoin in 1988 and his 5th dan in 1989. After serving as a Regional Director from 1989 to 1991, Scott Sensei was made one of four Branch Directors for Kokusai Budoin's United States operations. The Asian Martial Arts Studio is the Eastern United States Headquarters for Kokusai Budoin. With the other Branch Directors, he continues to oversee and coordinate Kokusai Budoin's activities in the United States. In 1994, he was awarded his 6th dan in the Karate-do Division and his 5th dan in the Aikido Division.

Over the course of his more than 30 years of training in the martial arts, Scott Sensei has been awarded a number of honorary titles in recognition of his accomplishments and abilities. Todd Sensei has given him the title of *So-Shihan* ("Chief Professor" or "Senior Teaching Model") in Karate-do and Shihan ("Full Professor" or "Teaching Model") in Aikido. Grandmaster Shimabukuro has also awarded him the title of *Shihan*. Kokusai Budoin has made him a Counselor for Kokusai Budoin's World Headquarters in Tokyo, Japan and awarded him the title of *Renshi* ("Assistant Professor" or "Expert"). Scott Sensei is also a licensed instructor in the United States, Japan, and Okinawa. In addition, he is an official Karate-do and Aikido examiner for both the Shudokan Martial Arts Association and Kokusai Budoin.

Scott Sensei is currently the Director of Training for the Asian Martial Arts Studio in Ann Arbor, Michigan. He continues to teach and oversee separate programs in Shorin Ryu and Shudokan Karate-do, Aikido, and both internal and external styles of Chinese Kung Fu, including Sil-Lum Hung-Gar, T'ai Chi Ch'uan, Bagua, and Hsing-Yi. In addition, Scott Sensei teaches Chinese lion dancing.

Although the Asian Martial Arts Studio offers instruction in many different martial arts, each is kept distinct and taught in accordance with the principles and traditions of that particular style. Scott Sensei has deliberately not blended the different styles together into a single, combined, martial art. Rather, he has gone to great lengths to maintain and teach each martial art in accordance with its traditional emphases. One reason for this is out of respect for the teachers and practitioners of the particular system. Another reason is his firm belief that any traditional martial art is a complete system within itself and that it is therefore important that one learn the entire system instead of drawing out disjointed pieces. Although there are many common principles, each martial art has its own unique specialties and advantages. Scott Sensei believes that one cannot fully appreciate or derive the maximum benefit from a particular style if one only selects and practices one's favorite techniques. For all of these reasons, the Asian Martial Arts Studio continues to preserve and teach each of the different styles of martial arts in their traditional manner.

One of the things I have always admired about Scott Sensei is his willingness to critically examine and re-examine his execution of karate and other martial arts techniques. This self-examination has enabled him to determine the most efficient and effective way to do a particular technique and to continually improve his own execution of it. In Scott Sensei, this critical analysis is combined with an understanding of the importance of practicing a technique over and over again.

Scott Sensei loves to do repetitions and knows that this is essential if one is to develop any level of proficiency. He is a perfectionist in this regard, yet recognizes and accepts that he will never fully perfect any technique. His love of the martial arts and his desire to spread them motivate him. He is always striving to improve himself and increase his knowledge so that he will be a more effective martial artist and teacher.

In June of 1991, I brought Scott Sensei to Atlanta to conduct special training seminars and teach classes at my school. At the end of the last class he taught, my students and I presented him with an engraved plaque in honor of his accomplishments. The inscription on the plaque summarizes the respect and gratitude I feel for Scott Sensei. It also captures the contribution that Scott Sensei has made to the martial arts and the example he has set for all of his students. The inscription reads:

KARL W. SCOTT III

YOU HAVE DEVOTED YOUR LIFE
TO THE ONGOING DEVELOPMENT
AND PROMULGATION OF THE MARTIAL
ARTS.
YOU HAVE INSPIRED US WITH YOUR
DEDICATED TRAINING
AND ENLIGHTENED US THROUGH YOUR
TEACHING.
THIS PLAQUE IS GIVEN TO SHOW OUR
DEEP APPRECIATION
AS WELL AS OUR COMMITMENT TO
UPHOLD THE STANDARDS YOU HAVE
ESTABLISHED.

The Okinawan Karate-do Club
Mark R. Moeller — Head Instructor
June 1, 1991

Y. JAY SANDWEISS SENSEI (b. 1953)

Y. Jay Sandweiss Sensei (Photo 8) began his karate training in September of 1974 at the Asian Martial Arts Studio, one year before he graduated as a philosophy major from the University of Michigan. His primary teacher was Scott Sensei. After a few years of training, Scott Sensei asked Sandweiss Sensei to join a group he was forming for special training. This group later became known as the "Tigers."

The Tigers were formed in response to an incident that occurred in a sparring class at the Asian Martial Arts Studio. A visitor from another school (with extensive martial arts experience) was sparring in a wild and overly aggressive manner. Scott Sensei noticed that several of the future Tigers, who were only green belts at the time, were somewhat intimidated and did not handle themselves effectively. Although a more senior student was easily able to defeat this individual, Scott Sensei decided that some of these lower-ranking students needed extra work to improve their confidence and abilities in fighting situations.

Scott Sensei selected only a handful of the junior students. He chose the ones he felt needed the most help and had demonstrated the heart and perseverance that the training he had in mind would require. Scott Sensei's guiding principle for the Tigers was to make the training significantly harder and more extreme than regular training. The Tigers met in secret at irregular hours and on weekends for intensive training sessions. These sessions emphasized *kata*, skill development drills, full-contact work, absorption training, and extensive physical conditioning. (For example, at one session the Tigers did 1,000 push-ups by interspersing *kata* practice with sets of 33 push-ups.) This approach proved to be very successful and the martial skills of the Tigers increased significantly.

Sandweiss Sensei applied himself vigorously and he never missed a meeting of the Tigers. Karate training, both with the Tigers and at the Asian Martial Arts Studio, was the central focus of Sandweiss Sensei's life during these years. He found work in Ann Arbor so he could continue his training after finishing school. He would train

for hours each day as he worked on improving his karate.

In 1977, Sandweiss Sensei was offered a unique opportunity. Knowing his interests in martial arts and the Orient, a relative asked him to spend three months observing and working in his factory on the island of Taiwan. After making arrangements to visit Grandmaster Shimabukuro's dojo in Okinawa before starting work, Sandweiss Sensei accepted his relative's offer.

He arrived in Okinawa in September of 1977 with a letter from Wong Sensei and Scott Sensei recommending his promotion to black belt. Over the course of the two week visit, Grandmaster Shimabukuro reviewed and corrected all of his *kata* and two-person exercises. He also awarded him his black belt. Near the end of his visit, Sandweiss Sensei made arrangements to live and work on Grandmaster Shimabukuro's chicken farm at the end of his three-month job in Taiwan.

After arriving at the small village on Taiwan where the factory was located, Sandweiss Sensei immediately established a karate training schedule for himself. In the evenings, he practiced his *kata* and karate techniques on the roof of the building where he lived. This was noticed by the villagers and word quickly spread.

Photo 8 — Sandweiss Sensei

Sandweiss Sensei's dedicated and consistent practice attracted the attention of Sifu Li, the local wushu (the Chinese word for "martial arts") master. Sifu Li was also the traditional Chinese doctor (specializing in acupuncture and Chinese herbs) for the 100,000-person village. Sifu Li sent an oral invitation to Sandweiss Sensei to visit his school, Sifu Li's Lung-Woo Chen (Sifu Li's Dragon-Tiger School). After meeting with Sandweiss Sensei and demonstrating a few techniques, Sifu Li offered him the opportunity to attend a class the next day.

Sandweiss Sensei readily accepted, but knew that he would have to "prove" himself worthy before he would be accepted as a student of Sifu Li. It is common among traditional Asian martial arts instructors to accept only a small number of students. Only those individuals who show a proper attitude, a strong desire to learn, and perseverance are accepted. In many instances, the instructor will use a procedure similar to the one Sifu Li used with Sandweiss Sensei to test prospective students before accepting them.

At the beginning of class, Sifu Li showed Sandweiss Sensei a basic technique involving interlocking arm circles. After making sure that he knew the technique well enough to practice it, Sifu Li left Sandweiss Sensei alone and went to work with the other students.

Sandweiss Sensei knew what he had to do. For the next 2 hours and until the class ended, he continued to practice the one technique over and over again. He resisted the temptation to practice his karate materials or to give in to the weariness in his arms. Meanwhile, Sifu Li continued to work only with the other students and did not appear to pay any attention to him. When the class was over, no comment on his efforts was made, but Sandweiss Sensei was invited back to attend a class the next day.

The second night was a repeat of the first night Again, Sifu Li showed Sandweiss Sensei one basic technique and left him alone to practice. Again, Sifu Li spent the entire two hour class working only with his other students. This time when the class was over, however, Sifu Li told Sandweiss Sensei that he could join the class as a regular student. Sandweiss Sensei had passed Sifu Li's test.

Sandweiss Sensei trained with Sifu Li virtually every day. Sifu Li was so impressed with Sandweiss Sensei's attitude and persistent practice that he began to teach him privately. He also refused to accept any additional money for these lessons. Because of his solid foundation in karate and his willingness to train hard, Sandweiss Sensei made rapid progress and learned a considerable amount.

Near the end of Sandweiss Sensei's time in Taiwan, Sifu Li began preparing his students for the national tournament for Taiwan. Sandweiss Sensei was working on an unarmed form and a weapons form. The tournament was held in a large stadium that held approximately 20,000 people. There were two simultaneous competition rings — one for weapons forms and one for unarmed forms. Out of the hundreds of contestants, Sandweiss Sensei was the only non-oriental.

As fate would have it, he was called to perform both his forms at the same time. He knew he would only be able to do one, but could not decide which one to do. His indecision did not last long. Sifu Li quickly came up to him and thrust the Tiger Fork into his hands. The Tiger Fork is a 5-foot wooden shaft with a large three-pronged end made out of steel. It was originally used for baling hay. Because of the weight of the Tiger Fork, the form Sandweiss Sensei performed required considerable upper body strength and firmly rooted stances.

As Sandweiss Sensei was standing in the ring and waiting for the signal to begin, he cleared his mind and prepared for his demonstration. He focused on one predominant thought: to show the judges and spectators the fighting spirit of Okinawan Karate-do. As he executed the form, he did not think about the individual movements, the judges, or the spectators. Instead, he imagined himself actually fighting a series of opponents in a life or death situation. When he finished the form's dramatic ending, he again became aware of his surroundings. As he looked around the stadium, he saw that the spectators were all on their feet and applauding loudly.

Because of the wide variety of styles participating, the tournament officials awarded nine first-place certificates for unarmed forms and nine first-place certificates for weapons forms. Sandweiss Sensei was awarded one of the first-place certificates for weapons forms by the nephew of Chiang Kai-shek.

Sandweiss Sensei left for Okinawa shortly after the tournament and arrived on Christmas Day in 1977. In Okinawa, he lived on Grandmaster Shimabukuro's chicken farm, which was located on the ocean north of Kin village. The accommodations were primitive. He lived in a metal hut that had only a small bedroom and a kitchen. All the plumbing was outdoors, and in the winter the shower would frequently freeze. The weather was not much better. In the winter it was cold, windy and damp. In the remaining months of the year, it was extremely hot and humid.

Sandweiss Sensei's workday started before dawn and continued until dark. He was responsible for feeding the chickens four times a day, providing for their care, and trimming and watering Grandmaster Shimabukuro's bonsai trees. To make matters worse, he soon found it was not exactly what he had expected. Although he had hoped to maximize his karate training time, the realities of living and working on a chicken farm made this difficult. The physical demands and hours of the job were very taxing. In addition, Grandmaster Shimabukuro was testing his spirit.

It was not until he had been working on the chicken farm for two weeks that Grandmaster Shimabukuro invited him to start attending classes. The classes lasted 2-3 hours a night, but most of the students would stay after class to continue practicing on their own. Once he started attending classes on a regular basis, Sandweiss Sensei soon excelled. After six weeks, Grandmaster Shimabukuro told him, "You have good heart, so now I will teach you." He began to instruct him privately on the techniques and *kata* of the entire Shobayashi Shorin Ryu system. In order to provide a place for Sandweiss Sensei to train in between his chores, Grandmaster Shimabukuro poured a rough concrete pad and installed two *makiwara* on the chicken farm. (A *makiwara* is a chest-high post which was embedded in the ground to provide resistance for punching and kicking practice as well as to toughen various parts of the body. The striking surface was originally padded with sheaved rice straw.) Sandweiss Sensei used this area to practice *kata*, karate drills and *makiwara* drills during the day between his work responsibilities.

Sandweiss Sensei put all of his heart, soul, and energy into his training. He made rapid progress and was awarded his 2nd dan in March of 1978. He was also made a part of Grandmaster Shimabukuro's demonstration team.

One day as Sandweiss Sensei was preparing for a demo at the local Marine Corps base, Grandmaster Shimabukuro told him that because he was now a 2nd dan, he would be breaking a stack of curved ceramic-type roof tiles at the demo. Sandweiss Sensei, who had never broken a single tile (or even a board) before, asked if he could practice before the demo. The answer was no. Grandmaster Shimabukuro explained that if he hurt his hand while practicing, he would be afraid and unable to break the tiles at the demo. He told Sandweiss Sensei that if he believed he would break the tiles, he would be able to do so.

A good student is one who trusts his teacher completely and without reservation. Sandweiss Sensei trusted Grandmaster Shimabukuro and did as he was instructed. He continued to work on his other materials for the demo and never attempted to break a tile. When it came time to break the 2-foot stack of tiles at the demo, Sandweiss Sensei's mind was clear. He focused on only one thought: that he was going to drive his hand all the way through the tiles to the ground. The tiles did not stand a chance. He stepped forward and cleanly broke all the tiles with a single punch (and without injuring his hand).

Sandweiss Sensei's Okinawan experience ended on a high note. Wong Sensei, Chan Sensei, Scott Sensei, and Zaremba Sensei all arrived in Okinawa. After living in foreign countries for almost nine months, Sandweiss Sensei was very glad to see them. In addition to conducting special training sessions, Grandmaster Shimabukuro also made arrangements for them to visit all of the major Okinawan karate schools and observe classes. Shortly before they returned to the

United States, Grandmaster Shimabukuro presented Sandweiss Sensei, Scott Sensei, and Zaremba Sensei certificates stating that they were certified, master instructors of Shorin Ryu Karate-do and thereby licensed to teach Shorin Ryu Karate-do.

After returning to Ann Arbor in the summer of 1978, Sandweiss Sensei was asked by Scott Sensei to become the Head Instructor of the University of Michigan Shorin Ryu Karate-do Club (the new name for the club originally started by Wong Sensei). The club grew under his leadership from 12 students (in January of 1979 when I started) to over 70 students in five years.

During this time period, Sandweiss Sensei took a job working nights so that he would have more time to devote to his training. He also became one of the senior Sil-Lum Hung-Gar Kung Fu instructors at the Asian Martial Arts Studio and began studying Aikido. In 1982, Sandweiss Sensei visited Grandmaster Shimabukuro during his visit to Seattle. Grandmaster Shimabukuro was very pleased that he was spreading Shorin Ryu as the Head Instructor of the University of Michigan Shorin Ryu Karate-do Club. He must have also been impressed with Sandweiss Sensei's karate proficiency because he double promoted him to 4th dan. (In addition to the promotions he received in Shorin Ryu over the years, Sandweiss Sensei also received identical promotions in Shudokan Karate-do from Todd Sensei. These promotions were approved upon the recommendation of Scott Sensei and generally occurred shortly after a Shorin Ryu promotion.)

It was during this period of his life that Sandweiss Sensei began to explore some of the healing arts. This was partially due to the influence of Sifu Li, who was both the village martial arts expert and the village doctor, and the acupressure/muscle-energy treatment he received for a knee injury that threatened his martial arts career. He became a certified instructor of the Touch for Health organization. This group taught the basics of acupressure and muscle-energy balancing work to laymen. After completing this training, Sandweiss Sensei started teaching Touch for Health seminars and working with people on a private basis.

His ability to help people with muscle strains and injuries caused his clientele to expand rapidly. Sandweiss Sensei was soon able to leave his night job and do acupressure and muscle-energy treatments on a full-time basis.

He applied the principles that had brought him success in his karate training — hard work, perseverance, and dedicated practice to improve oneself — to his study and practice of the healing arts. Once again, this earned him the opportunity to learn from an exceptional teacher. Sandweiss Sensei became the first person without either a chiropractic or medical degree to be accepted in the 100-hour Applied Kinesiology course created by the doctor who had helped his knee injury. (Applied Kinesiology is the medical discipline from which the Touch for Health techniques originated.) The course enabled Sandweiss Sensei to be more effective in both his teaching and his individual appointment sessions.

As he continued to work on people, Sandweiss Sensei found himself wanting to further expand his knowledge of the healing arts so he could help his clients more. In 1984, he started Osteopathic school at Michigan State University in Lansing, Michigan. Although he continued to run and teach the University of Michigan Shorin Ryu Karate-do Club for several years, the combination of the hour-and-a-half one-way commute and the demands of medical school made it impractical to continue. In 1987, Scott Sensei resumed full responsibilities for the club.

Sandweiss Sensei finished Osteopathic school and residency in 1989 and returned to Ann Arbor to setup his own practice. He has established a holistic practice that integrates traditional western and eastern medicine. In addition to osteopathic manipulation and traditional western medical techniques, he also incorporates acupuncture, nutrition, and Chinese herbal medicine in the treatment of his patients. He has also developed considerable expertise in the treatment of environmental sensitivities and allergies. Finally, a part of his practice is devoted to traditional family practice.

The return to Ann Arbor has also allowed Sandweiss Sensei to resume his training at the Asian Martial Arts Studio. In 1991, he was awarded his 5th dan in Shudokan Karate-do. He was awarded his 2nd dan in Aikido in 1992. He currently teaches both Karate-do and Aikido classes at the Asian Martial Arts Studio.

One of the things I admire most about Sandweiss Sensei is his ability to motivate the students in his classes. This is partially a function of the example he has set in his own life by diligently training and striving to improve himself, but it is also something more than that. His classes are filled with his spirit — a spirit that causes the students to perform to the best of their ability. One can almost feel an intangible energy in the room when he is teaching. His love of the martial arts is infectious, and it creates a feeling of excitement. Even in very large classes, he creates a personal "connection" with each of the students. In addition to his ability to project his spirit, he is also a patient teacher with a thorough understanding of the martial arts. The combination of this personal charisma and his technical proficiency make him an exceptional and inspirational teacher.

In my own life, Sandweiss Sensei has also been a significant motivating force. I always felt that he truly believed in me. I still remember the statement he made late one night as we were walking home from dinner after class. At the time, I had been training about two years and was a green belt. He told me I had a gift for teaching karate and that he knew someday I would be the Head Instructor of my own school. His confidence in me had a big impact on my life. I went on to earn my black belt and have become the Head Instructor of my own school. His faith in me has also inspired me to accomplish many other goals in karate and in other areas of life. I am grateful for all he has taught me, and I am honored to be able to call myself one of his students.

HOW TO LEARN KARATE

Before beginning the technical portion of this book, I want to offer my thoughts on the most efficient way to learn the karate techniques and exercises described in this book. Choose one or more techniques to practice. Start by doing ten repetitions of the technique during each practice session. If possible, practice every day. During each practice session, concentrate on doing each technique correctly and to the best of your ability. Do this by visualizing yourself executing the technique perfectly in your mind as your body does the physical motion. (It is also very beneficial to spend some time doing this kind of visualization training with your eyes closed and without moving.) In addition, strive to learn, understand, and apply the principles which make the individual techniques strong and effective.

During every other practice session, add another ten repetitions. Continue adding ten repetitions every other session until you reach the maximum number that can be completed during your available practice time. Another option is to stop increasing the number of repetitions when you reach one hundred per session.

Once you have established your own maximum number of repetitions, continue to do that many during each practice session until the technique can be done satisfactorily. At this point, reduce the number of repetitions to a "maintenance" level (such as twenty per session) and choose a different technique to practice using this process.

With this kind of diligent and consistent practice, you can learn all of the techniques and exercises in this book. Some will come easier than others, but nothing truly worthwhile ever comes easily. Try to be patient and not get frustrated. Remember that it is not innate ability that enables a person to learn karate. Rather, it is hard work and long hours of practice. Perseverance is the key. You can do it if you stick to it. I know.

PART II

Standing Bow — Rei

1. Start with the heels together and the feet pointing 45 degrees to either side of an imaginary line or plane (the "Center Line") extending straight forward from the center (i.e. the nose, throat, solar plexus, and groin) of the body. This stance is called *Musubi Dachi*. The arms are extended and straight along the sides of the body with the fingers extended (Fig. 1).

2. Bow by bending forward at the waist until the upper body is at approximately a 45 degree angle to the lower body while keeping the head, neck, and back in a straight line (Fig. 2). Pause briefly and then return to the upright starting position.

   To show respect for a senior student, the lower-ranking student should bow slightly lower and hold the bow slightly longer than the senior student. After the senior student starts to return to an upright position, the lower-ranking student may start to return to an upright position.

Figure 1

3. The eyes should look in the direction the head is facing as the bow is done. This means that two people bowing to each other do not look at each other's face. It is considered a sign of disrespect and distrust to look at the other person while bowing.

4. **Key Point:** Proper distancing and the use of peripheral vision while bowing enable the person to see and react to an attack before being struck. This is true even though the bowing person does not look at the other person's face. It is important to use peripheral vision and train awareness skills when bowing.

5. A person should bow when entering or leaving the formal training area or dojo. This helps prepare the mind to train with humility. It also shows respect and a proper attitude.

6. All formal individual and two-person exercises begin with a bow to show respect, humility, and a proper attitude.

Figure 2

Formal Kneeling Bow — Seiza

1. Start in *Musubi Dachi*. (The heels are together and the feet point 45 degrees to either side of the Center Line. The arms are extended and straight along the sides of the body with the fingers extended.) (Fig. 1)

2. Step backward with the left foot and go down onto the left knee by lowering the body equally with both legs. The left foot should be on the ball of the foot. The lower half of the right leg (i.e. from the knee to the heel) and the upper half of the left leg (i.e. from the hip to the knee) should be almost perpendicular to the ground (Fig. 3).

3. The right foot moves backward until it is even with the left foot and the right knee is resting on the ground like the left knee (Fig. 4). Both feet should be on the balls of the feet. The knees should be approximately 12 inches (3 fists) apart and the feet are approximately 8 inches apart. The head, neck, back, and the upper half of the legs should be in a straight line perpendicular to the ground. The hips should be tucked upward slightly.

4. The feet move toward each other until almost touching as the toes are extended backward until the body is resting on the tops of the feet. The upper body is then lowered backward until it is sitting on top of the heels and the upper and lower halves of the legs are touching each other (Fig. 5) (Fig. 6 next page). Each hand (with the fingers extended and together) rests on the top of its respective leg close to the hip joint. The head, neck, and back remain in a straight line perpendicular to the ground. This kneeling position is called *Seiza*.

Note: It is also acceptable to cross the feet so that the top of one foot is resting on the bottom of the other foot.

Figure 3

Figure 4

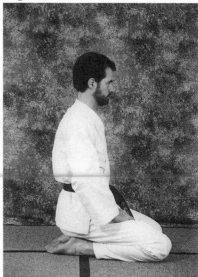

Figure 5

5. The upper body bends forward at the waist (while continuing to sit on the heels and keeping the upper and lower halves of the legs together) until the palms of both hands are resting on the ground. The left palm touches the ground first and then the right palm touches the ground. The palms are approximately 6 inches apart and 4 inches in front of the knees. They are also at approximately a 45 degree angle to each other (Fig. 7).

6. The upper body continues bending forward until the head, neck and back are in a straight line parallel to the ground and the nose is approximately 5 inches from the ground (Fig. 8) (Fig. 9 next page). Pause briefly and then return to *Seiza* position with the head, neck, and back in a straight line perpendicular to the ground. The right hand returns to the top of the leg first and then the left hand returns to the top of the leg.

Note: The eyes should look in the direction the head is facing as the bow is done. It is important to use peripheral vision and train awareness skills when bowing.

Figure 6 - Front View

Figure 7 - Front View

Figure 8

7. To return to a standing position, steps (2), (3), and (4) are done in reverse order: Both feet come up onto the balls of the feet (Fig. 10) and then the upper body rises forward until the head, neck, back, and the upper half of the legs are in a straight line perpendicular to the ground. The hips should be tucked upward slightly.

8. The right foot moves forward and rests on the sole as the right knee comes off the ground. The lower half of the right leg and the upper half of the left leg should be roughly perpendicular to the ground (Fig. 3).

9. Stand up (moving forward) using both legs equally and bring the left foot forward and even with the right foot. The heels of the feet are shoulder or hip width apart, whichever is wider. The legs are bent slightly at the knees and fifty percent of the weight is on each leg. This stance is called Natural Stance or *Hachiji Dachi*. Bring the left heel next to the right heel with the feet pointing 45 degrees to either side of the Center Line into a *Musubi Dachi*. The arms are extended and straight along the sides of the body with the fingers extended (Fig. 1).

10. The Formal Kneeling Bow is used as part of the traditional opening and closing of Karate-do classes.

Figure 9 - Front View

Figure 10

II. Warm-up Exercises

Key Principle

It is important to loosen the joints and stretch the muscles of the body before beginning to exercise. This reduces the chance of injury and enhances the body's performance.

Pushing Back on the Knees

1. Start in a natural standing position with the feet approximately shoulder-width apart and pointing straight forward.

2. Bend forward at the waist and place the hands directly on the front of the knee on the same side of the body as the hand.

3. Bend both knees as much as possible without lifting the heels off the ground and then straighten both knees while pushing backward with the hands. Do this 10 times.

Knee Rotations

1. Start in a natural standing position with the feet together and pointing forward.

2. Bend forward at the waist and place the hands directly on the front of the knee on the same side of the body as the hand.

3. Bend the knees slightly and make a horizontal circle with the knees. Do 10 clockwise circles and then do 10 counterclockwise circles.

Hip Rotations

1. Start in a natural standing position with the feet together and pointing straight forward.

2. Place the hands on the hip on the same side of the body as the hand.

3. Make a horizontal circle with the hips while attempting to keep the shoulders directly over the feet. Do 10 clockwise circles and then do 10 counterclockwise circles.

Neck Rotations

1. Start in a natural standing position with the arms relaxed.

2. Bend the head forward until the chin is almost touching the chest. Rotate the head completely around the neck until it returns to the starting position. Do 10 rotations clockwise and then do 10 rotations counterclockwise.

Shoulder Rotations

1. Start in a natural standing position with the feet together and pointing straight forward.

2. Extend both arms directly out to the side until fully extended and even with the shoulders.

3. Make a small vertical circle with both arms. Do 10 forward circles and then do 10 backward circles.

4. Make a large vertical circle with both arms. Do 10 forward circles and then do 10 backward circles.

Stomach Crunches

1. Lie on the ground face up with the arms extended along the sides of the body.

2. Bring the feet toward the hips until the bottom of the feet are resting on the ground and the knees are bent at approximately a 90 degree angle.

3. Slowly raise the upper body off the ground until the fingers touch the knees. Hold this position for five seconds and then slowly lower the upper body back to the ground. Do 20 stomach crunches.

Reverse Crunches

1. Lie on the ground face down with the arms extended above the head and out to the side slightly.

2. Slowly raise the upper and lower body off the ground as much as possible. Hold this position for five seconds and then slowly lower the upper and lower body back to the ground. Do 20 reverse crunches.

Push-ups

1. Bend down and place the palms of the hands on the ground about 12 inches in front of the feet and approximately shoulder-width apart.

2. Shift the weight to the arms and move the feet backward until the legs and back are in a straight line.

3. While keeping the legs and back in a straight line, bend the arms and lower the body toward the ground until the chest is a few inches above the ground. Raise the body to the starting position. Do 20 push-ups.

4. A traditional karate way to do push-ups is to make an Okinawan fist (described on page 67) and place the first two knuckles of the fist on the ground in a vertical fist position (the palms face each other). Do the push-ups from this position. This strengthens the wrist, toughens and conditions the knuckles and teaches the proper alignment of the forearm, wrist, and knuckles for executing a proper punch.

Stretching the Arms Backward

1. Start in a natural standing position with the feet approximately shoulder-width apart and pointing straight forward.

2. Bend both arms upward until each arm is bent at a 90 degree angle. Raise the arms until each elbow is directly in front of the shoulder on the same side of the body. (The elbows should also be even with the top of the shoulders.)

3. While keeping the elbows even with the top of the shoulders, move the elbows away from each other, out to the sides, and backward as far as is comfortably possible and then return to the starting position. Do this 20 times.

Stretching Forward and Backward

1. Start in a natural standing position with the feet together and pointing forward.

2. Exhale while extending the arms toward the ground and bending the upper body forward at the waist as much as possible to stretch out the muscles along the backs of the legs. Hold this position for 20-30 seconds and then return to a natural standing position.

3. Spread the feet apart to approximately twice the width of the shoulders and place the hands on the back of the hips. Inhale while bending the head and upper body backward as much as possible without losing balance to stretch out the muscles along the front of the body. Hold this position for 20-30 seconds and then return to a natural standing position.

4. Do this forward and backward stretch five times.

Quadriceps Stretch

1. Start in a natural standing position with the knees bent slightly.

2. While maintaining balance, bend one leg backward so the foot moves toward the hips and grasp the ankle. Pull the foot upward and toward the hip as much as possible to stretch out the quadriceps and other muscles along the front of the leg. Hold this position for 20-30 seconds and then return to a natural standing position. Note: Be sure to keep the supporting leg bent to maintain balance. It also helps to think of the body being centered over the hips.

3. Repeat these steps with the other leg. Do this stretch five times with each leg.

Front Kick Stretch

1. Start in a natural standing position with the knees bent slightly.

2. Raise one leg off the ground and grasp the front of the shin with both hands. Pull the knee toward the chest as much as possible. Hold this position for 20-30 seconds and then return to a natural standing position. Note: Be sure to keep the supporting leg bent to maintain balance. It also helps to think of the body being centered over the hips.

3. Repeat these steps with the other leg. Do this stretch five times with each leg.

III. Stances — Dachi

Key Principles For All Stances:

1. Always keep the shoulders over the hips — do not lean forward or backward with the upper body.

2. After changing from one stance to another, only the lower body should be different.

3. The eyes should look straight ahead so the head stays erect and does not bend forward.

Informal Attention Stance — Heisoku Dachi

1. The feet are together and point straight ahead (Fig. 11).

2. The legs are almost completely straight with only a slight bend in the knees.

3. Fifty percent of the weight is on each leg.

4. The head, neck, and back are in a straight line and the upper body does not lean forward or backward (Fig. 12).

Informal Attention Stance (feet out) — Musubi Dachi

1. The heels of the feet are together and the feet point 45 degrees to either side of the Center Line (Fig. 13).

2. The legs are almost completely straight with only a slight bend in the knees.

3. Fifty percent of the weight is on each leg.

4. The head, neck, and back are in a straight line and the upper body does not lean forward or backward.

Figure 11

Figure 12

Figure 13

Parallel Stance — Heiko Dachi

1. The feet are parallel, point straight ahead, and are shoulder or hip width apart, whichever is wider (Fig. 14).

2. The legs are bent slightly at the knees.

3. Fifty percent of the weight is on each leg.

4. The head, neck and back are in a straight line and the upper body does not lean forward or backward.

Open-leg or Natural Stance — Hachiji Dachi

1. The heels of the feet are shoulder or hip width apart, whichever is wider. The feet are turned outward at 30 degree angles to an imaginary line drawn straight forward from the inside edge of each heel (Fig. 15).

2. The legs are bent slightly at the knees.

3. Fifty percent of the weight is on each leg.

4. The head, neck and back are in a straight line and the upper body does not lean forward or backward.

Inverted Open-leg Stance — Uchi-hachiji Dachi

1. The toes of the feet are shoulder or hip width apart, whichever is wider. The feet are turned inward (as though pigeon-toed) at 45 degree angles to an imaginary line drawn straight backward from the inside edge of each big toe (Fig. 16).

2. The knees are bent and the hips are tucked upward as much as possible.

3. Fifty percent of the weight is on each leg.

4. The head, neck, and back are in a straight line and the upper body does not lean forward or backward.

Figure 14

Figure 15

Figure 16

Sumo Stance — Shiko Dachi

1. The feet are approximately two shoulder widths apart (approximately 36 inches) in a very wide stance. The feet are turned outward at 45 degree angles to an imaginary line drawn straight forward from the inside edge of each heel (Fig. 17).

2. The knees are pushed out to the sides (and over the toes) as much as possible.

3. Fifty percent of the weight is on each leg.

4. The head, neck, and back are in a straight line and the upper body does not lean forward or backward.

Horse Stance — Kiba Dachi

1. The feet are parallel, point straight ahead, and are approximately two shoulder (or hip, if wider) widths apart (approximately 36 inches) in a very wide stance (Fig. 18).

2. Fifty percent of the weight is on each leg.

3. The hips are tucked upward slightly.

4. The head, neck, and back are in a straight line and the upper body does not lean forward or backward (Fig. 19).

5. **Key Point:** The feet point straight ahead and the knees are pushed out to the sides (and over the toes) as much as possible.

Figure 17

Figure 18

Figure 19

Front Stance — Zen Kutsu Dachi

1. Start with the feet shoulder or hip width apart, whichever is wider. The foot of the leg that is to become the back leg of the front stance moves straight back until it is approximately 18-24 inches directly behind its starting position and approximately 24-30 inches diagonally behind the front foot. Both feet should now be on either side of the Center Line and an equal distance away from the Center Line (Fig. 20).

2. The front foot points straight forward with the front knee pushed forward over the toes. (It should not be possible to see the toes of the front foot (Fig. 21).)

3. The back foot is turned outward at a 45 degree angle to an imaginary line drawn straight forward from the inside edge of the back heel. The back leg is straight and tight, with the knee locked.

4. Sixty percent of the weight is on the front leg and forty percent of the weight is on the back leg.

5. The hips are tucked upward slightly.

6. The head, neck, and back are in a straight line and the upper body does not lean forward or backward.

7. **Key Point:** The front knee is pushed forward over the toes by the back leg.

Figure 20

Figure 21 — Side View

Cat Stance — Neko-ashi Dachi

1. The front toe is approximately 12-18 inches in front of the back heel.

2. The back foot is turned outward at a 45 degree angle to an imaginary line drawn straight forward from the inside edge of the back heel.

3. The back leg is bent as much as possible without causing the upper body to lean forward. Ninety percent of the weight is on the back leg and ten percent of the weight is on the front leg. The front leg is bent and rests lightly on the ball of the foot. The front foot points straight forward (Fig. 22).

4. **Key Point:** It should be possible to lift the front leg off the ground without disturbing the body's balance or having to shift the weight to the back leg.

5. The inside edges of the feet should be on opposite sides of the Center Line and the front foot should not be directly in front of the back foot. If the front foot is pulled straight back, it should just miss hitting the back heel.

6. The hips are shifted backward as though sitting on the edge of an imaginary chair, but the lower back curves forward slightly so that the head and shoulders are directly over the hips (Fig. 23).

7. **Key Point:** The body's weight and balance are centered over the back leg.

Figure 22

Figure 23

IV. Punches — Tsuki

Making an Okinawan Fist

1. The last three fingers of the hand (the little finger, the ring finger, and the middle finger) curl in tightly so that all three knuckles of the fingers are bent as much as possible.

2. The index finger bends in tightly, but the last knuckle (the knuckle closest to the fingernail) does not bend at all.

3. The thumb wraps around the fingers just above the last knuckle of the index finger and squeezes in tightly (Fig. 24).

4. When a punch is done, the wrist is straight so that the knuckles, the wrist, and the top of the forearm are all directly in line (Fig. 25).

Advantages of an Okinawan Fist

1. The wrist is harder to bend forward or backward than a fist made without keeping the last knuckle of the index finger straight. This prevents the wrist from buckling due to the recoil force upon impact and transfers more of the power of the punch into the object struck.

2. The middle knuckle of the index finger is less likely to be broken upon impact because it is not as exposed.

Figure 24

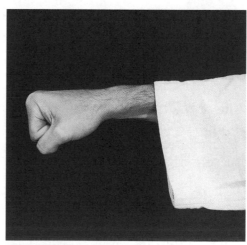

Figure 25

Doing a Punch

1. A standard punch starts with the hand at chamber position. Chamber position is where the hand is in a fist with the palm facing up and the little-finger edge of the fist presses against the floating ribs on the same side of the body as the hand (Fig. 26).

Figure 26

2. The arm should scrape along the side of the body lightly as the punch is coming out (Fig. 27).

3. The forearm twists and rotates completely over just before the end of the punch so that the palm is facing down when done. The arm is almost completely extended at the end of the punch, but there is a slight bend at the elbow (Fig. 28).

   Notes: There are some punches that do not turn completely over. When the hand is at chamber position in a fist, the palm of the hand always faces up.

Key Principles For Punches

1. The elbow is directly behind the fist throughout the entire punch.

2. The shoulders are pulled down at all times.

Figure 27

3. The hips and shoulders are square to the front (i.e. perpendicular to the Center Line) throughout the entire punch. If both arms are extended forward, each should extend the same distance. If one arm extends farther forward than the other, either the shoulders or the hips are not square to the front.

4. The arm does not lock at full extension. There should be a slight bend in it at the elbow.

5. All punches stop directly on the Center Line (Fig. 28).

6. The fist should be formed but not clenched. The muscles of the arm and hand stay relaxed until the very end of the punch when they contract to stop the punch and then immediately relax again. This is sometimes described as loose — tight — then loose again.

7. Generally, the non-punching hand is pulled back to chamber at the same time as the punching hand moves forward to increase power. The type of power that this generates is called returning power. In addition to increasing the power of the punch, this also puts the hand that is pulled back to chamber in a position where it can punch or execute a block, if necessary.

8. The striking surface for all standard punches is the knuckles closest to the wrist of the index and middle finger.

Figure 28

Types of Punches

1. Reverse Punch — *Gyaku Tsuki*

   a. This is a punch done with the hand on the same side of the body as the back leg of the particular stance (Fig. 29).

   b. "Reverse Punch" is also frequently used to describe a punch where the forearm rotates so that the palm of the punching fist faces down (toward the ground) when the punch is completed.

2. Lunge Punch — *Oi Tsuki*

   a. This is a punch done with the hand on the same side of the body as the front leg of the particular stance (Fig. 30).

   Note: Although this is called a "lunge" punch, the upper body should not lean forward when doing a lunge punch. The head, neck, and back should remain in a straight line.

Height of Punches for Individual Exercises

1. All high punches are at eye level.

2. All middle punches are at solar plexus level.

3. All low punches are at groin level.

   Note: When working with a partner during two-person exercises, the height of the punch is the partner's eyes, solar plexus, or groin level.

Figure 29

Figure 30

Snap or Speed Punches

1. A snap or speed punch starts with the punching hand on the Center Line and almost touching the breast bone. The other arm is almost fully extended in front of the breast bone and just slightly to the outside of the Center Line. Both hands are turned so that the knuckles are aligned vertically (Fig. 31).

2. The punching hand moves forward as the arm is extended (Fig. 32) and then pulls back to the starting position faster than it was extended (Fig. 31). The other hand is simultaneously pulled back to directly in front of the breast bone and then returns to its starting position.

   Note: The punching arm should not be fully extended and does not lock at the elbow.

Key Principle

The essence of snap or speed punches is to pull the hand back to the starting position faster than it is sent out. It is like cracking a whip.

Figure 31

Figure 32

V. Blocks — Uke

Upper Block — Jodan Uke

1. Executing the block:

   a. The arm (with the hand in a fist) comes up so that the hand comes close to the ear on the opposite side of the body with the palm facing in toward the body (Fig. 33).

   b. The forearm then rotates outward (*after* the arm crosses in front of the face) as the arm continues upward to the final position (Fig. 34).

   c. The elbow is below the fist throughout the entire block.

2. The blocking surface is first the inside edge (thumb side) of the forearm and then the outside edge (little-finger side) of the forearm. The blocking surface changes after the forearm rotates as it crosses in front of the face.

3. Completion Checkpoints:

   a. The bicep is in close to the ear (with the head remaining in an upright position);

   b. The palm faces forward (away from the body) with the wrist straight;

   c. The forearm is one fist's width away from the top of the forehead; and

   d. The arm is bent at a 45 degree angle to the ground.

4. **Key Point:** The Completion Checkpoints put the blocking arm in a position which makes it very difficult to pull the forearm straight down toward the ground. This is referred to as an unbendable arm position. It prevents the arm from collapsing when executing this block against a strong attack.

Key Principle

The elbow is below the fist throughout the entire block.

Figure 33

Figure 34

Middle (Outward) Block — Chudan Uke

1. Executing the block:

   a. The arm (with the hand in a fist) reaches across in front of the body so that the elbow is in front of the solar plexus and the hand is slightly above the waist (Fig. 35).

   b. The arm is then pulled across the body to the final position using the back and shoulder muscles (Fig. 36).

2. The blocking surface is the inside edge (thumb side) of the forearm.

3. Completion Checkpoints:

   a. The inside edge (thumb side) of the arm is even with the side of the body;

   b. The elbow is one fist's width away from the floating ribs (Fig. 37);

   c. The knuckles are even with the top of the shoulders;

   d. The arm is bent at a 90 degree angle; and

   e. The palm faces in (toward the shoulder) with the wrist straight.

4. **Key Point:** The Completion Checkpoints put the blocking arm in a position which makes it very difficult to push the fist toward, or pull the fist away from, the shoulder on the same side of the body as the blocking arm. This is referred to as an unbendable arm position. It prevents the arm from collapsing when executing this block against a strong attack.

Key Principle

The arm pulls across the body using the back and shoulder muscles instead of pivoting at the elbow.

Figure 35

Figure 36

Figure 37

Lower Block — Gedan Barai

1. Executing the block:

   a. The arm (with the hand in a fist) comes up so that the hand is next to the ear on the opposite side of the body (Fig. 38).

   b. The arm then moves downward and across in front of the body with a pendular motion to the final position (Fig. 39).

   Note: The palm faces inward throughout the entire block.

2. The blocking surface is the outside edge (little-finger side) of the forearm.

3. Completion Checkpoints:

   a. The outside edge (little-finger side) of the arm is even with the side of the body;

   b. The hand is one fist away from, and directly in front of, the center of the thigh on the same side of the body;

   c. The palm faces in (toward the body) with the wrist straight; and

   d. The arm is bent slightly at the elbow.

4. **Key Point:** The Completion Checkpoints put the blocking arm in a position which makes it very difficult to completely straighten the arm or break the arm at the elbow. This is referred to as an unbendable arm position. It prevents the arm from collapsing when executing this block against a strong attack. It also prevents the arm from being broken if the elbow is attacked.

Key Principle

The arm moves downward and across the front of the body in a pendular motion.

Figure 38

Figure 39

Cross Block — Soto Seiken Uke

1. Executing the block:

   a. The arm (with the hand in a fist) bends and comes straight up from chamber until the fist is near the shoulder on the same side of the body (Fig. 40).

   b. The arm then drives across and away from the body at a 45 degree angle (to the shoulders) to the final position (Fig. 41).

2. The blocking surface is the outside edge (little-finger side) of the forearm.

3. Completion Checkpoints:

   a. The elbow is one fist's width away from the solar plexus;

   b. The fist is even with, and directly in front of, the shoulder on the opposite side of the body;

   c. The arm is bent at a 90 degree angle; and

   d. If the thumb were extended straight back, it would point toward the shoulder on the same side of the body.

4. **Key Point:** The Completion Checkpoints put the blocking arm in a position which makes it very difficult to push the fist toward, or pull the fist away from, the shoulder on the same side of the body as the blocking arm. This is referred to as an unbendable arm position. It prevents the arm from collapsing when executing this block against a strong attack.

Key Principle

The arm drives across and away from the body at a 45 degree angle.

Figure 40

Figure 41

Circle Block — Shuto-ura Uke

1. Executing the block:

   a. With the fingers straight and extended, the arm comes up with the palm facing in (toward the body) so that the hand comes close to the ear on the opposite side of the body (like an openhanded Upper Block) (Fig. 42).

   b. The arm then makes an upward, vertical circle with the forearm rotating outward after it crosses in front of the face (Fig. 43).

   c. The arm then continues downward to the final position (Fig. 44).

2. The blocking surface is first the inside edge (thumb side) of the forearm and then the outside edge (little-finger side) of the forearm. The blocking surface changes after the forearm rotates as it crosses in front of the face.

Figure 42

Figure 43

Figure 44

3. Completion Checkpoints:

    a. The elbow is one fist's width away from the floating ribs (Fig. 45);

    b. The knuckles are even with the top of the shoulder;

    c. The arm is bent at a 90 degree angle;

    d. The outside edge (little-finger side) of the arm is even with the side of the body;

    e. The palm faces out (away from the shoulder) with the wrist straight; and

    f. The fingers are extended and together, with the thumb tucked in.

4. **Key Point:** The Completion Checkpoints put the blocking arm in a position which makes it very difficult to push the hand toward, or pull the fist away from, the shoulder on the same side of the body as the blocking arm. This is referred to as an unbendable arm position. It prevents the arm from collapsing when executing this block against a strong attack.

Note: The Completion Checkpoints are the same as for a Middle Block except for subsections (d), (e) and (f) above.

Figure 45

Key Principle

The arm makes a vertical (upward) circle as the forearm rotates outward.

Lifting Block — Ageru Uke

1. Executing the block:

   a. The arm (with the hand in a fist) reaches across in front of the body so that the elbow is in front of the solar plexus and the hand is slightly below the waist (Fig. 46).

   b. The arm then draws upward and across the front of the body in an arc (as though drawing a sword) to the final position (Fig. 47).

2. The blocking surface is the inside edge (thumb side) of the forearm.

3. Completion Checkpoints:

   a. The bicep is in close to the ear (with the head remaining in an upright position).

   b. The forearm is one fist's width away from the top of the forehead.

   c. The arm is bent at a 45 degree angle to the ground.

   d. The palm faces in (toward the body) with the wrist straight.

4. **Key Point:** The Completion Checkpoints put the blocking arm in a position which makes it very difficult to pull the forearm straight down toward the ground. This is referred to as an unbendable arm position. It prevents the arm from collapsing when executing this block against a strong attack.

   Note: The Completion Checkpoints are the same as for an Upper Block except for the difference listed in subsection (d) above.

Key Principle

The arm makes an arc and draws across the front of the body as it moves upward.

Figure 46

Figure 47

Alternating Blocks with Both Arms

1. The arm that completed the last block is called the "covering" arm because it covers and protects the vital targets located on the Center Line of the body (i.e. the eyes, nose, throat, solar plexus and groin).

2. The covering arm moves inward slightly either just before or at the same time as the blocking arm begins to block. The covering arm then returns to chamber position as the blocking arm executes the block.

3. The blocking arm is always on the outside (i.e. farther away from the body) and the covering arm (i.e. the arm that did the last block) is always on the inside.

4. The covering arm makes whatever adjustments are necessary so that the blocking arm can do a normal block.

5. The hand of the covering arm pulls back to chamber position for a punch as the blocking arm does the block.

Blocking Drill Sequence

1. Do two Upper Blocks, two Middle Blocks, two Cross Blocks, two Lower Blocks, two Circle Blocks, and two Lifting Blocks. The series then repeats itself.

2. The Blocking Drill starts with the right arm and then alternates arms.

Front Snap Kick — Mae Geri

1. Executing the kick:

   a. The kick begins in a Front Stance and is done with the back leg (Fig. 48)

   b. The knee of the back leg comes up as far as possible toward the chest with the heel pulled in toward the leg as much as possible. The ankle and toes are pointed and locked downward (Fig. 49). This is chamber position for a Front Snap Kick.

   Key Point: The knee should drive up toward the chest and the top of the leg should be at least parallel to the ground when chambering the Front Snap Kick.

Figure 48

Figure 49

c. The foot then moves straight forward as the leg is extended out (Fig. 50) and then the foot is pulled back to chamber position faster than it was extended (Fig. 49).

Key Point: The leg should not be fully extended and should not lock at the knee.

d. After pausing slightly, the leg returns to the ground in a Front Stance.

2. The kick may also be done in a Cat Stance with the front leg.

3. Striking Surfaces:

a. The striking surface is the top of the foot if the target is the groin.

b. If the toes are pulled back, the striking surface becomes the ball of the foot and other targets can be attacked. It is important that the ankle remain pointed downward and locked when the toes are pulled back (Fig. 51).

4. **Key Points:** The supporting leg should be bent to act as a shock absorber and maintain balance throughout the entire kick. This will be the front leg if the kick is done in a Front Stance and the back leg if the kick is done in a Cat Stance.

The head should remain at the same level throughout the entire kick. There should not be any rising up or sinking down during the kick. When the body rises up or sinks down, it telegraphs the kick. This allows an opponent to anticipate the kick and block or counterattack sooner.

If the kick is done properly so that balance is maintained, multiple kicks can be done from chamber position before the kicking leg returns to the ground.

Key Principles

The knee drives up toward the chest.

The foot is pulled back to chamber position faster than it is sent out. This is the essence of snap techniques. It is like cracking a whip.

Figure 50

Figure 51

Side Kick — Yoko Geri

1. Executing the kick:

   a. The kick begins in a Horse Stance turned sideways and is done with the front leg (Fig. 52).

   b. The back (supporting) leg slides forward until directly under the body. The foot of the supporting leg is at a 45 degree angle pointing away from the direction of the kick.

Figure 52

   c. The knee of the front leg comes up as far as possible toward the chest with the heel pulled in toward the leg as much as possible. The ankle and toes are pulled back and locked upward (Fig. 53). This is chamber position for a Side Kick.

   d. The upper body and hips rotate away from the direction of the kick and the foot is thrust out directly to the side (Fig. 54). The leg locks for a split second at full extension, and the foot is pulled back to chamber position (Fig. 53).

   Key Point: At full extension, the toes of the kicking foot (which have already been pulled back) should be parallel to, or below the level of, the heel of the kicking foot. If the toes of the kicking foot are above the level of the heel, then the correct muscles are not being used and one cannot generate much power with the kick.

   e. After pausing slightly, the leg steps straight down and the supporting (back) leg slides out (away from the direction kicked) and back into a Horse Stance.

2. The striking surface is the heel or outside edge of the foot.

3. The supporting (back) leg should be bent to act as a shock absorber and maintain balance throughout the entire kick.

4. The head should remain at the same level throughout the entire kick. There should not be any rising up or sinking down during the kick. When the body rises up or sinks down, it telegraphs the kick. This allows an opponent to anticipate the kick and block or counterattack sooner.

Figure 53

5. **Key Points:** The height of the side kick is the height where the toes can be kept at least parallel to the level of the heel. This is the correct form and will insure proper development of the side kick. The height of the kick can be raised as leg flexibility increases by practicing the kick and working on stretching exercises.

Key Principles

The leg is thrust out directly to the side and locked at full extension for a split second with the foot parallel to the ground.

This is a thrust technique and not a snap technique.

Figure 54

Roundhouse Kick — Mawashi Geri

1. Executing the kick:

   a. The kick begins in a Front Stance and is done with the back leg (Fig. 55).

   b. The foot of the supporting (front) leg is turned outward (away from the center of the body) on the ball of the foot as much as possible. The knee of the back leg is brought up to the side as high as possible with the heel pulled in toward the leg as much as possible. The ankle and toes are pointed downward and locked like they are for a Front Snap Kick (Fig. 56). This is chamber position for a Round-house Kick.

   Key Point: This is like chambering for a Front Snap Kick, but the kicking leg is rotated upward to the side until it is parallel to the ground.

Figure 55

   c. The foot then moves forward along a horizontal arc parallel to the ground (as the leg is extended out and straightens) (Fig. 57) and the foot is pulled back to chamber position faster than it was extended (Fig. 56).

   Key Points: The foot of the kicking leg should pass through the Center Line (as determined from the starting position in a Front Stance) as the kick is done.

   The leg should not be fully extended and should not lock at the knee.

   d. After pausing slightly, the leg returns to the ground in a Front Stance and the front foot pivots to return to its starting position in a Front Stance.

2. The kick may also be done in a Cat Stance with the front leg.

Figure 56

3. Striking surfaces:

   a. The striking surface is generally the top of the foot.

   b. If the toes are pulled back, the striking surface becomes the ball of the foot. It is important that the ankle remain pointed downward and locked when the toes are pulled back.

4. The supporting leg should be bent to act as a shock absorber and maintain balance throughout the entire kick. This will be the front leg if the kick is done in a Front Stance and the back leg if the kick is done in a Cat Stance.

Figure 57

5. Key Points: The head should remain at the same level throughout the entire kick. There should not be any rising up or sinking down during the kick. When the body rises up or sinks down, it telegraphs the kick. This allows an opponent to anticipate the kick and block or counterattack sooner.

If the kick is done properly so that balance is maintained, multiple kicks can be done from chamber position before the kicking leg returns to the ground.

For practice the kicking leg should be parallel to the ground in chamber position and throughout the entire kick. (Do not be discouraged if the kicking leg cannot be held parallel to the ground at first. This will occur gradually as leg flexibility increases by practicing the kick and working on stretching exercises. Strive to get as close to parallel as possible.) In application the chamber position and angle of the lower half of the leg is raised or lowered depending upon the target area.

Figure 58

Key Principles

The kick is essentially a front kick turned sideways so that the kicking leg moves in a horizontal arc parallel to the ground.

The foot is pulled back to chamber position faster than it is sent out. This is the essence of snap techniques. It is like cracking a whip.

Back Kick — Ushiro Geri

1. Executing the kick:

   a. The kick begins in a Cat Stance and is done with the front leg. The head turns and looks over the shoulder on the same side of the body (Fig. 58).

Figure 59

   b. The knee of the front leg comes up as far as possible toward the chest with the heel pulled in toward the leg as much as possible. The ankle and toes are pulled back and locked upward like they are for a Side Kick (Fig. 59). This is chamber position for a Back Kick.

   c. The upper body bends forward (in the opposite direction of the kick) at the waist as the foot is thrust directly backward (with the insides of the legs scraping together lightly) until the leg locks for a split second at full extension (Fig. 60).

      Key Point: At full extension, the toes of the kicking foot should be pointing down as much as possible.

   d. The upper body then straightens up as the foot is pulled back to chamber position (Fig. 59). After pausing slightly, the leg returns to the ground in a Cat Stance.

2. The striking surface is the heel of the foot.

Figure 60

3. The supporting (back) leg should be bent to act as a shock absorber and maintain balance throughout the entire kick. (The foot of the supporting leg may be pivoted slightly [until the toes are pointing straight forward] for greater balance.)

Key Principles

The upper body bends forward at the waist for power and balance as the heel thrusts backward.

This is a thrust technique and not a snap technique. The leg should lock at full extension for a split second before being pulled back to chamber.

VII. Punching Drill

Opening for the Punching Drill

1. Bow. The feet pivot so that the toes come together, both knees bend, the weight is shifted to the left leg, and the right foot slides straight out to the right into a Horse Stance.

2. The arms (which were extended along the sides of the body with the fingers extended and together) move forward and upward along a semicircular pathway until the hands cross in front of the eyes (with the right hand on top) (Fig. 61).

3. Both hands then pull back to chamber into Okinawan fists (palms up when done) (Fig. 62).

Note: It is important to maintain a good Horse Stance (with the hips tucked upward slightly) throughout the entire Punching Drill.

Figure 61

Figure 62

Punch Across the Body — Kagi Tsuki

1. Look 90 degrees to the left of the Center Line and punch across the body (at solar plexus level) with the right hand (Fig. 63).

2. Look 90 degrees to the right of the Center Line and punch across the body (at solar plexus level) with the left hand as the right hand pulls back to chamber (palm up when done).

3. **Key Point:** This punch is used at short ranges and the fist does not extend very far past the side of the body. Try not to overextend the arm or reach too far to the side.

4. Completion Checkpoints:

   a. The shoulders are pulled down, and the hips and shoulders stay square to the front (i.e. parallel to an imaginary line drawn between the heels). The upper body does not turn toward the side.

   b. The top of the forearm is parallel to the ground at solar plexus level and the palm faces down.

   c. The punch stops when the elbow of the punching arm is one fist away from the solar plexus.

Figure 63

Key Principle

The arm slides along the ribs and stomach as the fist comes around the front of the body.

Palm-Up Punch Middle — Ura Tsuki

1. Look straight along the Center Line and Palm-up Punch middle (i.e. at solar plexus level) with the right hand (without any forearm rotation) as the left hand pulls back to chamber (palm up when done) (Fig. 64).

2. Palm-up Punch middle with the left hand (without any forearm rotation) as the right hand pulls back to chamber (palm up when done).

3. Completion Checkpoints:

   a. The shoulders are pulled down, and the hips and shoulders stay square to the front.

   b. The fist is at the level of the solar plexus and is directly on the Center Line.

   c. There is no twisting or rotation of the forearm as the arm reaches full extension so the palm faces up when the punch is done.

   d. There should be a slight bend in the arm at the elbow when the arm is at full extension.

Key Principle

The elbow is pulled back behind the fist and the arm scrapes lightly along the side of the body.

Figure 64

Reverse Punch Middle — Chudan Tsuki

1. Reverse Punch middle with the right hand as the left hand pulls back to chamber (palm up when done) (Fig. 65).

   A Reverse Punch is a punch that twists and rotates completely over just before the arm reaches full extension so that the palm is facing down when done.

2. Reverse Punch middle with the left hand as the right hand pulls back to chamber (palm up when done).

3. Completion Checkpoints:

   a. The shoulders are pulled down, and the hips and shoulders stay square to the front.

   b. The fist is at the level of the solar plexus and is directly on the Center Line.

   c. The palm faces down when the punch is done.

   d. There should be a slight bend in the arm at the elbow when the arm is at full extension.

Key Principle

The elbow is pulled back behind the fist, the arm scrapes lightly along the side of the body, and the fist rotates over just before the arm reaches full extension.

Figure 65

Vertical Punch High — Tate Tsuki

1. Vertical Punch high (i.e. at eye level) with the right hand as the left hand pulls back to chamber (palm up when done) (Fig. 66).

   A Vertical Punch is a punch that does not rotate completely over as the punch is completed. Instead, the rotation stops when the palm is facing sideways (and toward the Center Line) and the knuckles are aligned vertically.

2. Vertical Punch high with the left hand as the right hand pulls back to chamber (palm up when done).

3. Completion Checkpoints:

   a. The shoulders are pulled down and the hips and shoulders stay square to the front.

   b. The fist is at the level of the eyes and is directly on the Center Line.

   c. The knuckles are aligned vertically. If the thumb were extended, it would point straight up.

   d. There should be a slight bend in the arm at the elbow when the arm is at full extension.

Key Principle

The elbow is pulled back behind the fist, the arm scrapes lightly along the side of the body, and the fist rotates to a vertical position just before the arm reaches full extension.

Figure 66

Roundhouse Punch — Mawashi Tsuki

1. Roundhouse Punch high (i.e. at temple level) with the right hand as the left hand pulls back to chamber (palm up when done) (Fig. 67).

   A Roundhouse Punch is done by dropping the hand until it is next to the leg and then loosely swinging the hand and arm upward along a semicircular pathway until it stops even with the temples. The arm and forearm rotate inward (as the hand moves toward the temple) until the knuckles are aligned vertically with the thumb pointing straight down if it were extended.

2. Roundhouse Punch high with the left hand as the right hand pulls back to chamber (palm up when done).

3. **Key Point:** The arm should be relaxed as it moves along the semicircular pathway until just before it reaches temple level and then the arm muscles contract to stop the arm's movement. Without this relaxation, it is impossible to generate the maximum power from this punch. This type of power is sometimes referred to as "loose/heavy" or "whipping" power.

Figure 67

4. Completion Checkpoints:

   a. The shoulders are pulled down (as much as possible) and the hips and shoulders stay square to the front.

   b. The fist is at the level of the temples and is directly on the Center Line.

   c. The knuckles are aligned vertically. If the thumb were extended, it would point straight down.

   d. There should be a slight bend in the arm at the elbow when the arm is at full extension.

Key Principle

The arm stays relaxed as it loosely swings upward along the semicircular pathway.

Double Reverse Punch — Morote Tsuki

1. Pull the left hand back to chamber (palm up when done) and do a Double Reverse Punch middle with both hands. The hands are one fist apart when done and both palms face down (Fig. 68). *Kiai* as the Double Reverse Punch is done.

2. A *kiai* is a loud sound caused by contracting the diaphragm to force air out of the mouth. It is used to increase the power of the technique (augmentation with breath power), to contract the stomach muscles in case of a counterattack, and to startle and momentarily freeze an opponent.

3. Completion Checkpoints:

   a. The shoulders are pulled down, and the hips and shoulders stay square to the front.

   b. The fists are at the level of the solar plexus, are one fist apart, and are almost on the Center Line.

   c. The palms face down when the punches are done.

Figure 68

   d. There should be a slight bend in the arms at the elbows when the arms are at full extension.

4. This punch is called Morote-tsuki.

Key Principle

Each arm does a proper Reverse Punch. In other words, both elbows are pulled back behind the fists, the arms scrape lightly along the sides of the body, and the fists rotate over just before the arms reach full extension. Do not allow the elbows to flare out or the effectiveness of these punches will be greatly reduced.

Recovery — No-te

1. The right leg slides in until the right foot is next to the left foot (with the knees still bent) as the arms cross in front of the chest. The right arm is on the outside (i.e. farthest away from body), and each hand is almost directly in front of the shoulder on the opposite side of the body (Fig. 69).

Figure 69

2. Both knees straighten to slowly return the body to an upright position as each hand moves downward until it is one fist away from the front of its respective leg.

3. The feet pivot on the heels until pointing 45 degrees to either side of the Center Line and the arms (with the fingers extended and together) come to the sides of the body. The Punching Drill is completed with a bow.

VIII. Itosu Lines

Key Principle

Learning to get power from the rotation of the hips in an upright stance.

Opening for Itosu lines

1. Bow. Step out into "Ready Position" (*Yoi*):

   a. The feet step out (left foot first, then the right foot) into a Natural Stance (*Hachiji Dachi*) with the feet shoulder or hip width apart and the knees only slightly bent. The feet are turned outward at 30 degree angles to an imaginary line drawn straight forward from the inside edge of each heel.

   b. The hands form Okinawan fists and each hand moves to a position one fist away from the front of its respective leg.

   c. The arms are extended, but there is a slight bend at the elbow (Fig. 70).

2. Move to Formal Starting Position *(Kamae-te)*:

   a. The right foot turns until pointing 45 degrees to the right of an imaginary line (the Back-Heel Line) extending straight forward from the inside edge of the right heel (Fig. 71).

   b. The left foot circle steps forward by tracing a counter-clockwise arc along the ground with the ball of the foot until the left foot is parallel with the right foot, and the feet are approximately 10-16 inches apart (Fig. 72). (This will be called Itosu Stance in this book.)

Figure 70

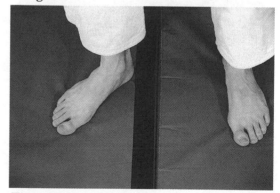
Figure 71

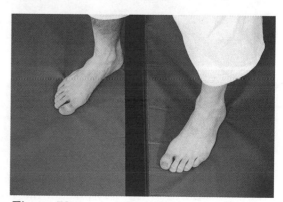
Figure 72

Key Point: The inside edges of both feet are at a 45 degree angle to the Back-Heel Line, and the big toe of the front foot (the left foot to start) should not cross the Back-Heel Line.

c. The right wrist crosses over and rests on top of the left wrist in front of the groin.

d. Throughout the entire series, the head faces directly forward and the eyes look straight ahead along the Back-Heel Line (even though the body is turned 45 degrees to the Back-Heel Line) (Fig. 73).

First Itosu Line — Itosu Shodan

1. Moving Forward - The First Series:

    a. Do the Opening for the *Itosu* lines (*Kamae-te*).

    b. The arms fold upward against the chest. The left arm is now on the outside (i.e. farther away from the body than the right arm) (Fig. 74).

    c. The left arm does a Circle Block as the right hand (in a fist) simultaneously pulls back to chamber (palm up when done) (Fig. 75).

    Key Point: The Circle Block finishes with the palm of the hand facing directly forward and the outside edge (little-finger side) of the arm parallel to the Back-Heel Line and even with the left side of the body.

    d. The left fingers squeeze into a fist as though grabbing another person's sleeve.

Figure 73

Figure 74

Figure 75

e. The hips and shoulders rotate counterclockwise as one unit as the right hand punches middle (i.e. at solar plexus level and directly along the Center Line) with a Reverse Punch (palm down when done) as the left hand simultaneously pulls back to chamber (palm up when done) (Fig. 76).

2. Moving Forward - The Second and Subsequent Series:

a. The left foot pivots 90 degrees counterclockwise on the heel. The inside edge of the left foot is now 45 degrees to the left of a Back-Heel Line running from the inside edge of the left heel.

b. The right foot then circle steps forward by tracing a clockwise arc along the ground with the ball of the foot until parallel with the left foot in an Itosu Stance.

Figure 76

c. The arms stay in approximately the same position that they were in at the conclusion of the preceding step (the left hand is at chamber and the right (forward) arm continues to point straight forward along the Center Line) during the step forward (Fig. 77).

d. The hips and shoulders rotate clockwise as one unit as the left arm Reverse Punches middle (palm down when done) as the right hand simultaneously pulls back to chamber (palm up when done) (Fig. 78).

e. Repeat the preceding steps (a-d) with alternating sides of the body as many times as desired. There is no minimum or maximum number of forward steps. The number of steps taken will be determined by the size of the training area and the amount of time available to practice.

Key Points: All punches should be directly on the Center Line when they are completed.

The head faces directly forward and the eyes look straight ahead throughout the entire Moving Forward series. This is true even though the body is turned 45 degrees sideways before the punch.

Figure 77

Figure 78

Key Principles

Figure 79

a. On all punches the hips and shoulders rotate together as one unit. This rotation is done with a simultaneous push and pull of the hips. This rotation of the hips is augmented by the rear leg pushing the hip forward while the front leg simultaneously pulls it backward. The hips lock-in after rotating to the point where the hips (and the shoulders) are perpendicular to the Back-Heel Line.

b. It is critical that the punch begin with the hips/shoulders starting their rotation before the arm begins to punch. This is necessary to generate the maximum amount of power.

c. The Moving Forward Series incorporates the principle of starting a technique with the larger, stronger muscles (i.e. the legs, hips and shoulders) and finishing the technique with the smaller, quicker muscles (i.e. the upper arm and forearm).

3. Moving Back:

a. Footwork:

The front foot comes straight back (without hitting the back heel) and becomes the back leg of a Cat Stance.

Figure 80

The foot that becomes the front foot of the Cat Stance pivots on the ball of the foot (with the heel moving away from the Center Line) after completing the step back.

Key Point: The foot should not move along a circular pathway to go around the back heel. If it is necessary to move in a circular pathway, then the preceding stance was too narrow.

Note: The Moving Back series may begin on either side of the body, but always starts with the front leg of the last Itosu Stance moving backward and becoming the back leg of the Cat Stance.

b. Blocking Series:

The Blocking Series begins after completing the step back into a Cat Stance.

The arm on the same side of the body as the front leg (after completing the step back) does a Middle Block (Fig. 79).

Figure 81

On the first step, this will be the arm that just punched.

On subsequent steps, the arm that just blocked moves inward slightly to cover (Fig. 80) and simultaneously pulls back to chamber (palm up when done) as the opposite arm does a Middle Block (Fig. 81).

The blocking arm should be on the outside (i.e. farther away from the body than the covering arm) when the arms cross.

Key Points: After completing the step back into the next Cat Stance, the Middle Block is always done with the arm on the same side of the body as the front leg.

4. Recovery — *No-te*:

a. Shift the weight to the front leg and circle the back foot forward by tracing forward along the ground with the ball of the foot until the feet are even with each other and are shoulder width apart. The hips and shoulders should be perpendicular to the Center Line.

b. Both knees straighten to return to a Natural Stance as the arms cross and return to Ready Position (Fig. 70).

c. Bring the left foot next to the right foot as the arms extend fully and come next to the sides of the body with the fingers extended and pointing downward.

d. The *Itosu* line is completed with a bow.

Key Principles

After stepping back into the first Cat Stance, the body should not rise up or drop down when moving backward — the head should remain at the same height throughout each step.

On the Moving Back Series, complete the step back into the Cat Stance before doing the block. ("Step, then block.") This is critical. If the block is done before the step is completed, the body is not grounded and stable. Against a strong attack, the block will pull the body off balance and will not deflect the attack. In addition to the block not being effective, this off balance position leaves one vulnerable to another attack and unable to counterattack effectively. This principle is one of the most important to understand and apply.

Second Itosu Line — Itosu Nidan

1. Do the opening for the *Itosu* lines.

2. Moving Forward:

    This is the same as Moving Forward for *Itosu Shodan* (including the Circle Block with the left arm) except the Reverse Punch (palm down when done) is a high punch (i.e. at eye level) (Fig. 82).

Figure 82

3. Moving Back:

    a. The footwork is the same as the footwork for *Itosu Shodan*.

    b. Blocking Series — The First Series:

    The hand that punched last when moving forward turns over (palm up) and pulls back toward chamber position while the other hand (in a fist with palm down) moves to on top of the hand that punched last and together they continue to pull back into a *kamae* position at chamber (Fig. 83). A *kamae* is a pause that occurs when the hands are in a resting or fixed position.

    This *kamae* is on the same side of the body as the front leg of the Cat Stance and is done only on the first backward step. There is a brief pause in this *kamae*.

    The arm with the palm of the hand facing up does a middle level Cross Block (with the hand in a fist) as the other hand simultaneously pulls back to chamber on the other side of the body (palm up when done) (Fig. 84).

Figure 83

Figure 84

The arm that just did the Cross Block then does a Lower Block (Fig. 85).

c. Key Point: The Lower Block starts from the ending position of the Cross Block instead of its regular starting position by the ear.

d. Blocking Series — The Second and Subsequent Series:

The arm that just did the Lower Block "covers" by moving inward slightly in front of the groin on the step backward into the next Cat Stance. There is no *kamae*. The hand at chamber position moves to directly in front of the shoulder on the same side of the body in preparation for the Cross Block (Fig. 86).

The arm with the hand in front of the shoulder does a middle level Cross Block (with the hand in a fist) as the other hand pulls back to chamber (palm up when done) (Fig. 87).

The arm that just did the Cross Block does a Lower Block (Fig. 88 next page).

Note: After completing the step back into the next Cat Stance, the Cross Block and Lower Block are always done with the arm on the same side of the body as the front leg.

Figure 85

Figure 86

Figure 87

Key Principles

a. After stepping back into the first Cat Stance, the body should not rise up or drop down when moving backward — the head should remain at the same height throughout each step.

b. Remember to step, then block.

c. There is a kamae only on the first step.

d. Make sure the Cross Block is a distinct block before doing the Lower Block. The two blocks should not blend together.

e. The Lower Block starts from the ending position of the Cross Block instead of its regular starting position by the ear.

4. Recovery — *No-te*

The Recovery is the same as the Recovery for Itosu Shodan.

Third Itosu Line — Itosu Sandan

1. Do the opening for the *Itosu* lines (*Kamae-te*).

2. Moving Forward — The First Series:

a. The arms fold upward until in front of the chest. The left arm is now on the outside (i.e. farther away from the body than the right arm) (Fig. 89).

b. Without twisting the hips, the left arm does an Upper Block as the right hand pulls back to chamber (palm up when done) (Fig. 90).

Figure 88

Figure 89

Figure 90

3. Moving Forward — The Second and Subsequent Series:

a. Circle step forward into an Itosu Stance.

b. The arm that just blocked (now the covering arm) comes down in front of the face (palm facing in) (Fig. 91) and pulls back to chamber (palm up when done) as the other arm (i.e. the one with the hand that was at chamber position) does an Upper Block (Fig. 92).

Key Points: The arm doing the Upper Block is on the outside (i.e. farther away from the body than the covering arm) when the arms cross in front of the chest.

There is no hip and shoulder twist.

c. Repeat the preceding steps (a-b) with alternating sides of the body as many times as desired. There is no minimum or maximum number of forward steps. The number of steps taken will be determined by the size of the training area and the amount of time available to practice.

Figure 91

Key Principles

a. Remember to step, then block.

b. There is no hip twist on any of the steps.

c. The elbow is always below the fist as the Upper Block is executed.

d. The head faces directly forward and the eyes look straight ahead throughout the entire Moving Forward Series. This is true even though the body is turned 45 degrees sideways as the block is done.

4. Moving Back:

a. The Footwork is the same as the Footwork for Itosu Shodan.

b. Blocking Series:

After completing the step back into a Cat Stance, the arm that just blocked (now the covering arm) comes down in front of the face (palm facing in) (Fig. 93) and pulls back to chamber (palm up when done) as the other arm (i.e. the one with the hand that was at chamber position) does a Lifting Block (Fig. 94 next page).

Note: The arm doing the Lifting Block is on the outside (i.e. farther away from the body than the covering arm) when the arms cross.

Figure 92

Figure 93

Key Principles

a. After stepping back into the first Cat Stance, the body should not rise up or drop down when moving backward — the head should remain at the same height throughout each step.

b. Remember to step, then block.

c. After completing the step back into the next Cat Stance, the Lifting Block is always done with the arm on the same side of the body as the front leg.

5. Recovery — *No-te*

The Recovery is the same as the Recovery for *Itosu Shodan*.

Figure 94

Key Principle

Learning to move forward and backward in a Front Stance.

Opening for Kiyan Shodan and Kiyan Nidan

1. Bow. Step out into Ready Position (*Yoi*):

   a. The feet step out (left foot first, then the right foot) into a Natural Stance (*Hachiji Dachi*) with the feet shoulder or hip width apart and the knees only slightly bent. The feet are turned outward at 30 degree angles to an imaginary line drawn straight forward from the inside edge of each heel.

   The hands form Okinawan fists and each hand moves to one fist away from the front of its respective leg.

   b. The arms are extended, but there is a slight bend at the elbow (Fig. 95).

   Note: This is the same as the opening for the *Itosu* lines.

2. Move to Formal Starting Position (*Kamae-te*):

   a. Both knees bend and the weight is shifted to the left leg. The right foot circles back into a left-foot forward Front Stance (*Zen Kutsu Dachi*) by tracing a counterclockwise arc along the ground with the ball of the right foot.

   b. After completing the step, the left arm does a Middle Block as the right hand simultaneously pulls back to chamber (palm up when done) (Fig. 96) (Fig. 97).

Figure 95

Figure 96

Figure 97 Side View

First Kiyan Line — Kiyan Shodan

1. Do the Opening for *Kiyan Shodan* and *Kiyan Nidan* (*kamae-te*).

2. Moving Forward:

   a. Circle step forward into a Front Stance:

   Turn the left foot 45 degrees counterclockwise on the heel. The left foot is now 45 degrees to the left of an imaginary line (the "Front-Heel Line") extending straight forward from the inside edge of the left (front) heel.

   The right foot circle steps forward by tracing a clockwise arc along the ground with the ball of the right foot into a right-foot forward Front Stance. The right foot comes next to the left foot (Fig. 98) and moves forward and out to the side along a crescent-shaped arc until it is the proper width and distance forward for a Front Stance.

Figure 98

   b. After completing the circle step forward, the right arm punches middle (i.e. at solar plexus level) with a Lunge Punch (palm down when done) as the left hand simultaneously pulls back to chamber (palm up when done) (Fig. 99) (Fig. 100).

   Key Point: Make sure the front knee is pushed forward over the toes.

   c. Circle step forward with the left foot into a left-foot forward Front Stance. After completing the step, the left arm does a Lunge Punch middle (palm down when done) as the right hand simultaneously pulls back to chamber (palm up when done).

Figure 99

   d. Repeat steps (a-c) with alternating sides of the body as many times as desired. There is no minimum or maximum number of forward steps. The number of steps taken will be determined by the size of the training area and the amount of time available to practice.

Key Principles

   a. After completing the circle step forward into a Front Stance, the Lunge Punch is always done with the arm on the same side of the body as the front leg.

   b. All punches should be directly on the Center Line when they are completed.

Figure 100 Side View

c. After the initial circle step backward into a Front Stance, the body should not rise up or drop down when moving forward. The head should remain at the same height throughout each step. If the body rises up or drops down when moving, this telegraphs the punch and will reduce the amount of power transferred from the legs to the arms.

d. When circle-stepping forward in *Kiyan Shodan* and *Kiyan Nidan*, the punch starts as the front foot stops and the knee starts to move forward over the toes. This timing for the punch ensures that the body is grounded and stable when the punch makes contact with an opponent. It also transfers the momentum and power of the body's forward motion into the punch.

3. Moving Back:

a. Circle step backward into a Front Stance:

The weight is shifted to the back leg.

The front foot then circle steps backward by tracing an arc along the ground with the ball of the foot into a Front Stance. The foot moving backward comes next to the other foot and moves backward and out to the side along a crescent-shaped arc until it is the proper width and distance backward for a Front Stance.

After the foot has completed the step backward, the new front foot pivots inward on the heel until it is pointing straight forward.

Key Point: Make sure the Front Stance is not too narrow and that the front knee is pushed forward over the toes.

Note: The Moving Back series may begin on either side of the body, but always starts with the front leg of the last Front Stance moving backward and becoming the back leg of the next Front Stance.

b. Blocking Series — The First Series:

While circle stepping backward, the hand that punched last turns over (palm facing up) and pulls back toward chamber position while the other hand (in a fist with the palm facing down) comes on top of the hand that punched last (Fig. 101), and together they continue to pull back into a *kamae* position at chamber. (*Kamae* with palms facing each other.) (Fig. 102) (Fig. 103).

Figure 101

Figure 102

Figure 103 - Side View

Both hands are now on the same side of the body as the back leg of the Front Stance.

After a brief pause, the arm on the same side of the body as the front leg of the Front Stance (i.e. the one with the hand on top of the other hand and the palm facing down) does a Middle Block (Fig. 104) (Fig. 105).

The blocking arm stays in the Middle Block position while the other hand does a reverse punch middle (palm down when done) (Fig. 106) (Fig. 107).

c. Blocking Series — The Second and Subsequent Series:

While circle stepping backward, the hand of the arm that did the Middle Block pulls back toward chamber position (with the palm facing up) while the hand that punched (with the palm facing down) comes on top of the hand of the blocking arm, and together they continue to pull back into a *kamae* position at chamber. (*Kamae* with palms facing each other.)

Key Point: Both hands are now on the same side of the body as the back leg of the Front Stance.

After a brief pause, the arm on the same side of the body as the front leg of the Front Stance (i.e. the one with the hand on top of the other hand and the palm facing down) does a Middle Block.

The blocking arm *stays* in the Middle Block position while the other hand does a Reverse Punch middle (palm down when done).

d. **Key Points on Moving Back:** After completion of the circle step backward into a Front Stance, the blocking arm is always on the same side of the body as the front leg.

There is a *kamae* with the palms facing each other on every step and the hand of the blocking arm is always on top.

The arm that blocked does not return to chamber as the other arm punches.

All punches should be directly on the Center Line when they are completed.

Figure 104

Figure 105 Side View

Figure 106

Figure 107 Side View

Key Principles

a. The body should not rise up or drop down when moving backward — the head should remain at the same height throughout each step.

b. Complete the step back into the Front Stance before doing the block. ("Step, then block.") This is critical. If the block is done before the step is completed, the body is not grounded and stable. Against a strong attack, the block will pull the body off balance and will not deflect the attack. In addition to the block not being effective, off-balance position leaves one vulnerable to another attack and unable to counterattack effectively. This principle is the same as the Key Principle for moving back in the *Itosu* Lines and is one of the most important principles to understand and apply.

4. Recovery — *No-te*

a. Circle the back foot forward by tracing along the ground with the ball of the foot until the feet are even with each other and are shoulder width apart (with the hips and shoulders perpendicular to the Center Line).

b. Both knees straighten to return to a Natural Stance as the arms cross and return to Ready Position (Fig. 108).

c. Bring the left foot next to the right foot as the arms extend fully and come next to the sides of the body with the fingers extended and pointing downward.

d. The *Kiyan* Line is completed with a bow.

Second Kiyan Line — Kiyan Nidan

1. Do the Opening for the *Kiyan Shodan* and *Kiyan Nidan* (*Kamae-te*).

2. Moving Forward is the same as Moving Forward for *Kiyan Shodan* except the Lunge Punch (palm down when done) is a high punch (i.e. at eye level) (Fig. 109) (Fig. 110).

3. Moving back:

a. The footwork is the same as the footwork for *Kiyan Shodan*.

b. Blocking Series — The First Series:

While circle stepping backward, the hand that punched last turns over (palm facing up) and pulls back toward chamber position while the other hand (in a fist with the palm facing up) comes on top of the hand that punched last, and together they continue to pull back into a *kamae* at chamber. (*Kamae* with palms facing up.) (Fig. 111) (Fig. 112)

Figure 108

Figure 109

Figure 110 Side View

Figure 111

Figure 112 - Side View

Both hands are now on the same side of the body as the back leg of the Front Stance.

After a brief pause, the arm on the same side of the body as the front leg of the Front Stance (i.e. the one with the hand on top of the other hand and the palm facing up) does an Upper Block (Fig. 113) (Fig. 114).

The blocking arm *stays* in the Upper Block position while the other hand does a Reverse Punch high (palm down when done) (Fig. 115) (Fig. 116).

Figure 113

c. Blocking Series — The Second and Subsequent Series:

While circle stepping backward, the hand of the arm that did the Upper Block pulls back toward chamber position (with the palm facing up) while the hand that punched (with the palm facing up) comes on top of the hand of the blocking arm, and together they continue to pull back into a *kamae* at chamber. (*Kamae* with palms facing up.)

Both hands are now on the same side of the body as the back leg of the Front Stance.

After a brief pause, the arm on the same side of the body as the front leg of the Front Stance (i.e. the one with the hand on top of the other hand and the palm facing up) does an Upper Block.

The blocking arm *stays* in the Upper Block position while the other hand does a Reverse Punch high (palm down when done).

Figure 114 Side View

d. **Key Points for Moving Back:** After completion of the circle step backward into a Front Stance, the blocking arm is always on the same side of the body as the front leg and it does not pull back to chamber as the other hand does the punch.

There is a kamae with the palms facing up on every step and the hand of the blocking arm is always on top.

The arm that blocked does not return to chamber as the other arm punches.

Figure 115

All punches should be directly on the Center Line when they are completed.

4. Recovery — *No-te*

The Recovery is the same as the Recovery for *Kiyan Shodan.*

Figure 116 Side View

Third Kiyan Line — Kiyan Sandan

1. Opening

    a. Bow. Step out into Ready Position (*Yoi*).

2. Moving Forward:

    a. Step forward with the left foot and go down onto the right knee by lowering the body equally with both legs.

    The right foot should be on the ball of the foot.

    The lower half of the front leg (i.e. from the knee to the heel) and the upper half of the back leg (i.e. from the hip to the knee) should be almost perpendicular to the ground.

    b. The left fist comes up by the right ear as the body is lowered (Fig. 117) (Fig. 118).

    c. The left arm does a Lower Block (which stops directly above the left knee) as the right hand simultaneously pulls back to chamber (palm up when done) (Fig. 119) (Fig. 120).

    Key Point: The body should be lowered equally with both legs. In this manner the strength of both legs is utilized and the body is more balanced.

    The blocking arm (the left arm on the first step) is on top of the arm returning to chamber (the right arm on the first step) as they cross.

Figure 117

Figure 118 Side View

Figure 119

Figure 120 Side View

d. The right hand does a Reverse Punch (palm down when done) to the height of the solar plexus while resting on one knee. The left hand simultaneously pulls back to chamber (palm up when done) (Fig. 121) (Fig. 122).

e. Stand up (moving forward) using both legs equally and bring the right foot (the back foot) forward and even with the left foot to return to a Natural Stance. The arms cross and return to Ready Position.

f. Step forward with the right foot and repeat steps (a-e) on the opposite side of the body.

g. Repeat steps (a-f) on alternating sides of the body as many times as desired. There is no minimum or maximum number of forward steps. The number of steps taken will be determined by the size of the training area and the amount of time available to practice.

3. Moving Back:

a. Step backward with the right foot and go down onto the right knee by lowering the body equally with both legs.

The right foot should be on the ball of the foot.

The lower half of the front leg (i.e. from the knee to the heel) and the upper half of the back leg (i.e. from the hip to the knee) should be almost perpendicular to the ground.

Note: The Moving Back series always begins with the right foot moving backward and the body being lowered onto the right knee.

Figure 121

Figure 122 Side View

b. The left hand (with fingers extended and left together) comes up by the right ear (Fig. 123). The left arm does a lower *Shuto* (Knife-Hand or Sword-Hand) Block (an open-handed Lower Block) which stops directly above the left knee. The right hand simultaneously pulls back to chamber is a fist (palm up when done) (Fig. 124) (Fig. 125).

Key Point: The blocking arm (the left arm on the first step) is on top of the arm retruning to chamber (the right arm on the first step) as they cross.

Figure 123 - Side View

Figure 124 - Side View

Figure 125

c. The right hand (with fingers extended and together) does a *nukite* thrust (a spear-hand thrust with the thumb-side up) to the height of the solar plexus while on one knee. The left hand simultaneously pulls back to chamber in a fist (palm up when done) (Fig. 126) (Fig. 127).

d. Stand up (moving backward) using both legs equally and bring the left foot (the front foot) backward and even with the right foot to return to a Natural Stance. The arms cross and return to Ready Position.

e. Step backward with the left foot and repeat steps (a-d) on the opposite side of the body.

f. Repeat steps (a-e) on alternating sides of the body as many times as desired.

4. Recovery — *No-te*

a. Bring the left foot next to the right foot as the arms extend fully and come next to the sides of the body with the fingers extended and pointing downward.

b. The *Kiyan* line is completed with a bow.

5. **Key Points:** After lowering the body onto one knee, the blocking arm is always on the same side of the body as the front leg. The hand of the blocking arm stops close to the top of the knee that is not touching the ground.

Figure 126 - Side View

The foot on the same side of the body as the knee that rests on the ground should be on the ball of the foot when (1) lowering the body, (2) performing the block and punch, and (3) raising the body.

The Moving Forward Series always begins with the left foot moving forward and the body being lowered onto the right knee.

The Moving Back Series always begins with the right foot moving backward and the body being lowered onto the right knee.

Key Principles

a. Both legs should be used equally when lowering the body onto one knee and when raising the body up to Natural Stance.

b. When Moving Forward and Moving Back, the block should start its downward descent just as the knee touches the ground. This transfers the momentum and power of the body's weight dropping into the block. It makes the block much stronger because it utilizes the mass of the entire body instead of just the arms and shoulders.

Figure 127

X. Two-Person Exercises — Ippon Kumite

Introduction and General Principles

The Japanese name for the Two-Person Exercises described in this book is *Ippon Kumite*. *Ippon Kumite* means "one-step sparring or fighting." It is used to refer to two-person drills that involve a prearranged attack and counter series. (In the beginning, these generally involve a single punch or kick, hence the name "one-step" sparring.)

The main purpose of *Ippon Kumite* is to isolate a specific technique so that it can be learned and then practiced over and over again. If done properly, the techniques are all distanced so that no contact is made even if an attack is blocked late, ineffectively, or not at all. The advantage of this is that one can concentrate on doing the technique correctly and with the proper application of principles, instead of only trying to block as quickly as possible to avoid being hit. As one becomes more proficient and confident, the speed is increased gradually until the series are done at or close to full speed.

Ippon Kumite are very effective self-defense techniques. My teachers used to say that against an untrained opponent, one should only have to use one *Ippon Kumite* series to defend oneself. *Ippon Kumite* are also the building blocks for higher level fighting skills and techniques. They teach essential skills related to timing, distance, and fighting rhythms. When *Ippon Kumite* have been practiced enough to develop "body knowledge," the body will naturally use the correct techniques from these series in a fighting situation.

Individual practice of the *Ippon Kumite* is very beneficial. If a partner is not available, practice the moves for both the Attacker and the Defender alone. This will help the body learn and internalize the specific movements of the different exercises. When the exercises are later done with a partner, more attention and concentration can be placed on interacting with the partner instead of on remembering the movements of the exercises. Individual practice of Ippon Kumite can also significantly increase speed because there is no waiting for an attack or counter.

Key Principles for Practicing Ippon Kumite

The correct attitude is one of cooperation and not competition. Treat your partner's body as though it were your own. The attitude should be: I will lend you my body to improve your technique if you will lend me your body to improve mine.

Always look at your partner's eyes and use your peripheral vision to "take in" their whole body. The eyes will "telegraph" or give away when a person is going to attack.

Be sure to keep your hips and shoulder square when punching and blocking. This prevents you from overextending on the punches and keeps you in a better position to counterattack or block. It will also make your techniques faster if you eliminate unnecessary hip and shoulder movements.

Begin by practicing slowly and with good control. Correct form, precision, and accuracy are much more important than speed. If you use correct form, you are doing the series in the most efficient and effective manner. Speed will come with repetitions, but the proper body positions will not be developed unless you concentrate on doing each series correctly as you practice it. You therefore have to do the drills at a speed that allows you to concentrate in this manner. This will also make practice safer and reduce the possibility of accidentally injuring your partner.

The speed should be increased very gradually and only as each partner becomes more comfortable and adept at the series. The more skillful partner should work at the level and speed of the less skillful partner. Speed will come naturally and more quickly with this kind of practice. This enables the less skillful partner to improve more rapidly than if the series are done at a pace which is too fast. (This is also advantageous to the more skillful partner because it will ultimately make the other person a better partner in a shorter period of time.)

The muscles of the body should by as relaxed as possible. Relaxed does not mean limp or weak. Rather, it means eliminating unnecessary tension that wastes energy and slows movements. The right amount of tension is the minimum amount necessary to complete the block or attack. This is a feeling that develops naturally after training and practicing with different partners.

Relaxation is the key to speed. The contraction of incorrect muscles inhibits the freedom of motion. This can be felt with a simple experiment.

Start with one arm extended in a completed punch position and the other arm in chamber position. Contract the muscles of the arms as much as possible and clench the fists tightly. While maintaining these contractions, try to throw a hard, fast punch. Now repeat this experiment and keep the arms relaxed and the fists formed, but not clenched. The arms and fist stay relaxed until the fist reaches full extension. The muscles then contract to stop the forward motion of the fist and immediately relax again. (When actually striking an opponent, there is no contraction at the end of the punch. The resistance of the opponent's body is what stops the punch as the force and energy of the punch are channeled through the opponent's body. The contraction is necessary for individual work to prevent injury due to hyperextension of the arm [or leg].) The longer the contraction is held at the end of the punch, the more that energy is wasted and the longer it will take before the arms can start another movement. The feeling should be loose — tight — then loose again. When this is done correctly, the second punch will be considerably harder and faster.

Most beginners use considerably more energy and tension than is required. Strive to eliminate this unnecessary tension and be more relaxed. To learn to do this naturally and effectively, both partners should concentrate on relaxing while executing the various techniques of the *Ippon Kumite*. If one partner starts becoming tight, there is a strong tendency for the other partner (if inexperienced) to become tight as well. As one becomes more experienced, however, one learns to remain relaxed even when his partner or opponent is tight.

Two-Person Exercises — Ippon Kumite

1. All Two-Person Exercises (including *Ippon Kumite*) start with the partners bowing to each other (Fig. 128).

2. The height of punches for Two-Person Exercises:

   a. All high punches should be at the level of the other person's eyes (Fig. 129).

Figure 128

Figure 129

b. All middle punches should be at the level of the other person's solar plexus (Fig. 130).

c. All low punches should be at the level of the other person's groin (Fig. 131).

3. The palm of the hand at chamber should always face up and the palm of the punching hand should always face down (except for the Vertical Punch done in the Lower Series).

4. The contact points for both partners during the blocking of a punch are the forearms between the wrist and the elbows.

5. Standard Attacking Position (*Gedan Barai*) for Right Side Series ("Right Hand Attacking Position"):

a. Start in Ready Position.

b. The right foot circles back into a left-foot forward Front Stance.

c. After the step is completed, the left arm does a Lower Block as the right hand pulls back to chamber (palm up when done).

Figure 130

Figure 131

6. Proper distancing for the High-Middle-Low Series and the Singles, Doubles, and Triples Series:

a. Both partners start in Ready Position facing each other and extend one arm straight forward with the fingers extended. The distance is correct when the person with the longer arm can just touch the other person's chest (Fig. 132).

b. Key Point: It is essential that both partners keep their hips and shoulders square to the front or the distance will be incorrect.

c. Without changing the distance, the Attacker steps back into Right Hand Standard Attacking Position to begin the particular Ippon Kumite (Fig. 133).

Figure 132

Figure 133

High — Middle — Low Series

Defender

1. Start in Ready Position (Fig. 134).

Figure 134

2. Circle step back into a left-foot forward Front Stance and do a left Upper Block to block the Attacker's right punch as the right hand pulls back to chamber (palm up when done) (Fig. 135).

Figure 135

3. Circle step back into a right-foot forward Front Stance and do a right Middle Block to block the Attacker's left punch as the left hand pulls back to chamber (palm up when done) (Fig. 136).

Figure 136

4. Circle step back into a left-foot forward Front Stance and do a left Lower Block to block the Attacker's right punch as the right hand pulls back to chamber (palm up when done) (Fig. 137).

5. The Defender then becomes the Attacker and the series repeats.

Figure 137

Attacker

1. Start in Right Hand Attacking Position (Fig. 134).

2. Circle step forward into a right-foot forward Front Stance and do a right Lunge Punch high (palm down when done) as the left hand pulls back to chamber (palm up when done) (Fig. 135).

3. Circle step forward into a left-foot forward Front Stance and do a left Lunge Punch middle (palm down when done) as the right hand pulls back to chamber (palm up when done) (Fig. 136).

4. Circle step forward into a right-foot forward Front Stance and do a right Lunge Punch low (palm down when done) as the left hand pulls back to chamber (palm up when done) (Fig. 137).

5. The Attacker then becomes the Defender and the series repeats.

Notes: The Attacker always punches with the hand that is on the same side of the body as the front leg of the Front Stance (after the step forward is completed).

The Defender always blocks with the arm that is on the same side of the body as the front leg of the Front Stance (after the step backward is completed).

Training Variations

1. One Count/One Step: One count for each step and punch.

2. One Count/Three Steps: One count for all three steps and three punches.

3. Locking In: The Attacker "locks-in" on each punch and tries to prevent the Defender from blocking the arm. This tests the effectiveness of the blocks.

4. Defender's Eyes Closed:

    a. The Attacker starts in Right Hand Attacking Position and the Defender starts in a right-foot forward Front Stance. The Defender extends the right arm and makes contact with the outside edge of the Attacker's left forearm.

    Note: This position is the same as the position that the original Attacker and the original Defender finish in after the original Defender has punched low and the original Attacker has blocked the punch with a left Lower Block.

    b. The Defender's eyes close while the Attacker's remain open. The Attacker initiates each of the three steps and punches. The Defender must respond (i.e. step back and block at the appropriate times) based on the tactile sensations received through the arms.

    c. Key Points: The Defender steps backward when the Defender feels the Attacker's arm moving toward the Defender and the Defender executes the block when the Defender feels the Attacker's arm moving away from the Defender. The Defender feels the Attacker's arm move away when the Attacker pulls the non-punching arm back to chamber. The speed of the block is calculated by feeling how fast the Attacker's arm is pulled back. The faster the pullback, the faster the block will have to be to intercept the punch at the right time. With practice and enough repetitions, the appropriate timing is felt and the body automatically uses the right speed for the block. Start slowly and gradually increase the speed.

    It is the Attacker's responsibility to never hit the Defender. This allows the Defender to concentrate on the tactile sensations without the fear of being hit. When one is afraid, there is a natural tendency to become tense and contract the muscles. As the arm muscles are contracted, sensitivity decreases and it is harder to feel the movement and speed of the Attacker's arm.

    Relaxation of the Defender's arm is very important. This greatly enhances sensitivity. Try this experiment. Contract the forearms tightly and clench one fist. With the other hand, lightly run one finger up and down the forearm. Do the same thing again but this time keep the forearm and fist relaxed. When this is done correctly, the relaxed arm will be able to detect a much lighter touch and will therefore provide more tactile information about the other person's movements. Remember that relaxation does not mean limp. The fist should be formed, but not clenched.

    Try to maintain contact with the Attacker's arm as much as possible. When the contact is broken (as it is just before the blocking arm intercepts the punch), there is no longer any tactile information to interpret. This is sometimes referred to as "sticking with" an opponent.

    d. After the Defender has finished the Lower Block, the Defender's eyes open and the Attacker's eyes close. The Defender becomes the Attacker, and the Attacker becomes the Defender. The series then repeats.

5. Down and Back: One count for all six steps and six punches.

Singles — Upper Part Series on the Right Side

Defender

1. Start in Ready Position (Fig. 138).

Figure 138

2. Circle step back into a left-foot forward Front Stance and do an Upper Block with the left arm to block the Attacker's punch as the right hand pulls back to chamber (palm up when done) (Fig. 139).

Figure 139

Then do a right Reverse Punch high (palm down when done) as the left hand pulls back to chamber (palm up when done) (Fig. 140).

3. After completing the punch, recover by moving the right leg and returning to Ready Position.

Figure 140

Attacker

1. Start in Right Hand Attacking Position (Fig. 138).

2. Circle step forward into a right-foot forward Front Stance and do a right Lunge Punch high (palm down when done) as the left hand pulls back to chamber (palm up when done) (Fig. 139).

3. After the Defender completes the punch and starts to recover, move the right leg and return to Right Hand Attacking Position.

Blocking Variations

1. Open-Hand Cross Block (the fingers are extended and together) (Fig. 141).

   Note: After blocking with an Open-Hand Cross Block, the Defender's counter punch is above, or on top of, the Attacker's arm (Fig. 142).

2. Circle Block (Fig. 143).

Memory Aid

The Defender does the last punch on Single Series and initiates the recovery.

Figure 141

Figure 142

Figure 143

Doubles — Upper Part Series on the Right Side

Defender

1. Start in Ready Position.

2. Circle step back into a left-foot forward Front Stance and do an Upper Block with the left arm to block the Attacker's punch as the right hand pulls back to chamber (palm up when done) (Fig. 144).

Figure 144

Then do a right Reverse Punch high (palm down when done) as the left hand pulls back to chamber (palm up when done) (Fig. 145).

Figure 145

3. After the Attacker completes the punch and starts to recover, move the right leg and return to Ready Position.

Figure 146

Attacker

1. Start in Right Hand Attacking Position.

2. Circle step forward into a right-foot forward Front Stance and do a right Lunge Punch high (palm down when done) as the left hand pulls back to chamber (palm up when done) (Fig. 144).

3. Block the Defender's punch with the left arm (using the same block that the Defender used) as the right hand pulls back to chamber (palm up when done) (Fig. 145).

Then do a right Lunge Punch high (palm down when done) as the left hand pulls back to chamber (palm up when done) (Fig. 146).

4. After the punch, recover by returning to Right Hand Attacking Position.

Blocking Variations

1. Open-Hand Cross Block (the fingers are extended and together).

    Note: Both the Defender's punch and the Attacker's counter punch are above, or on top of, the other person's arm.

2. Circle Block.

Memory Aids

1. The Defender does the same thing as for Singles Series.

2. The Attacker does the same thing as for Singles Series but adds another block and punch.

3. The Attacker does the last punch on Doubles Series and initiates the recovery.

Triples — Upper Part Series on the Right Side

Defender

1. Start in Ready Position.

2. Circle step back into a left-foot forward Front Stance and do an Upper Block with the left arm to block the Attacker's punch as the right hand pulls back to chamber (palm up when done) (Fig. 147).

3. Do a right Reverse Punch high (palm down when done) as the left hand pulls back to chamber (palm up when done) (Fig. 148).

4. Block the Attacker's punch with the left arm (using the same block used to block the Attacker's first punch) as the right hand pulls back to chamber (palm up when done) (Fig. 149).

Then do a right Reverse Punch high (palm down when done) as the left hand pulls back to chamber (palm up when done) (Fig. 150).

5. After completing the punch, recover by moving the right leg and returning to Ready Position.

Figure 147

Figure 148

Figure 149

Figure 150

Attacker

1. Start in Right Hand Attacking Position.

2. Circle step forward into a right-foot forward Front Stance and do a right Lunge Punch high (palm down when done) as the left hand pulls back to chamber (palm up when done) (Fig. 147).

3. Block the Defender's punch with the left arm (using the same block that the Defender used) as the right hand pulls back to chamber (palm up when done) (Fig. 148).

4. Do a right Lunge Punch high (palm down when done) as the left hand pulls back to chamber (palm up when done) (Fig. 149).

5. After the Defender starts to recover, move the right leg and return to Right Hand Attacking Position.

Blocking Variations

1. Open-Hand Cross Block (the fingers are extended and together).

   Note: Both the Attacker's counter punch and the Defender's counter punches are above, or on top of, the other person's arm.

2. Circle Block.

Memory Aids

1. The Attacker does the same thing as for Doubles Series.

2. The Defender does the same thing as for Singles Series but adds another block and punch.

3. The Defender does the last punch on Triples Series and initiates the recovery.

Singles — Middle Part Series on the Right Side

Defender

Attacker

1. Start in Ready Position (Fig. 151).

Figure 151

1. Start in Right Hand Attacking Position (Fig. 151).

2. Circle step back into a left-foot forward Front Stance and do a Middle Block with the left arm to block the Attacker's punch as the right hand pulls back to chamber (palm up when done) (Fig. 152).

Figure 152

2. Circle step forward into a right-foot forward Front Stance and do a right Lunge Punch middle (palm down when done) as the left hand pulls back to chamber (palm up when done) (Fig. 152).

Then do a right Reverse Punch middle (palm down when done) as the left hand pulls back to chamber (palm up when done) (Fig. 153).

3. After completing the punch, recover by moving the right leg and returning to Ready Position.

Figure 153

3. After the Defender completes the punch and starts to recover, move the right leg and return to Right Hand Attacking Position.

Blocking Variations

1. Open-Hand Cross Block (the fingers are extended and together) (Fig. 154).

   Note: After blocking with an Open-Hand Cross Block, the Defender's counter punch is under, or beneath, the Attacker's arm (Fig. 155).

2. Circle Block (Fig. 156)

Memory Aid

The Defender does the last punch on Single Series and initiates the recovery.

Figure 154

Figure 155

Figure 156

Doubles — Middle Part Series on the Right Side

Defender

1. Start in Ready Position.

2. Circle step back into a left-foot forward Front Stance and do a Middle Block with the left arm to block the Attacker's punch as the right hand pulls back to chamber (palm up when done) (Fig. 157).

Figure 157

Then do a right Reverse Punch middle (palm down when done) as the left hand pulls back to chamber (palm up when done) (Fig. 158).

Figure 158

3. After the Attacker completes the punch and starts to recover, move the right leg and return to Ready Position.

Figure 159

Attacker

1. Start in Right Hand Attacking Position.

2. Circle step forward into a right-foot forward Front Stance and do a right Lunge Punch middle (palm down when done) as the left hand pulls back to chamber (palm up when done) (Fig. 157).

3. Block the Defender's punch with the left arm (using the same block that the Defender used) as the right hand pulls back to chamber (palm up when done) (Fig. 158).

Then do a right Lunge Punch middle (palm down when done) as the left hand pulls back to chamber (palm up when done) (Fig. 159).

4. After the punch, recover by returning to Right Hand Attacking Position.

Blocking Variations

1. Open-Hand Cross Block (the fingers are extended and together).

   Note: Both the Defender's punch and the Attacker's counter punch are below, or underneath, the other person's arm.

2. Circle Block.

Memory Aids

1. The Defender does the same thing as for Singles Series.

2. The Attacker does the same thing as for Singles Series but adds another block and punch.

3. The Attacker does the last punch on Doubles Series and initiates the recovery.

Triples — Middle Part Series on the Right Side

Defender

Attacker

1. Start in Ready Position.

2. Circle step back into a left foot forward Front Stance and do a Middle Block with the left arm to block the Attacker's punch as the right hand pulls back to chamber (palm up when done) (Fig. 160).

Figure 160

1. Start in Right Hand Attacking Position.

2. Circle step forward into a right-foot forward Front Stance and do a right Lunge Punch middle (palm down when done) as the left hand pulls back to chamber (palm up when done) (Fig. 160).

3. Do a right Reverse Punch middle (palm down when done) as the left hand pulls back to chamber (palm up when done) (Fig. 161).

Figure 161

3. Block the Defender's punch with the left arm (using the same block that the Defender used) as the right hand pulls back to chamber (palm up when done) (Fig. 161).

4. Block the Attacker's punch with the left arm (using the same block used to block the Attacker's first punch) as the right hand pulls back to chamber (palm up when done) (Fig. 162).

Figure 162

4. Do a right Lunge Punch middle (palm down when done) as the left hand pulls back to chamber (palm up when done) (Fig. 162).

Then do a right Reverse Punch middle (palm down when done) as the left hand pulls back to chamber (palm up when done) (Fig. 163).

5. After completing the punch, recover by moving the right leg and returning to Ready Position.

Figure 163

5. After the Defender starts to recover, move the right leg and return to Right Hand Attacking Position.

Blocking Variations

1. Open-Hand Cross Block (the fingers are extended and together).

   Note: Both the Attacker's counter punch and the Defender's counter punches are below, or underneath, the other person's arm.

2. Circle Block.

Memory Aids

1. The Attacker does the same thing as for Doubles Series.

2. The Defender does the same thing as for Singles Series but adds another block and punch.

3. The Defender does the last punch on Triples Series and initiates the recovery.

Memory Aid for all Right Side Series

The right leg of both the Attacker and the Defender is the one that moves, and all punches are done with the right hand by both the Attacker and the Defender.

Singles, Doubles and Triples — Left Side Series

The Series are identical to the ones listed above except they are done with the opposite side of the body.

Memory Aid for all Left Side Series

The left leg of both the Attacker and the Defender is the one that moves, and all punches are done with the left hand by both the Attacker and the Defender.

Lower Series — Right Side Series

Standard Attacking Position

1. Start in Ready Position.

2. The right foot circles back into a left-foot forward Front Stance.

3. After the step is completed, the arms (with the hands in fists) extend down and out to the sides as though holding two heavy buckets of water (Fig. 164).

4. Proper distancing for the Lower Series:

   a. The Defender stands in Ready Position.

   b. The Attacker extends the right leg toward the Defender's belt knot as though doing a Front Snap Kick and holds the leg at almost full extension. The distance is correct when the Attacker can touch the Defender's belt knot with a slight bend in the knee (Fig. 165).

Figure 164

Figure 165

First Lower Series

1. Attacker

   a. Start in Standard Attacking Position.

   b. Do a Front Snap Kick with the right leg to the level of the Defender's belt knot. After the Defender blocks the kick with a Lower Block, the leg returns to its original position in Standard Attacking Position.

2. Defender

   a. Start in Ready Position.

   b. Circle step back into a left-foot forward Front Stance and do a Lower Block with the left arm to block the Attacker's right kick as the right hand pulls back to chamber (palm up when done) (Fig. 166).

Figure 166

   c. **Key Points:** It is important that the blocking arm does not extend beyond the side of the body. Once the blocking arm has deflected the Attacker's kick past the Defender's body (which occurs when the blocking arm is even with the side of the body), any further movement of the blocking arm past the side of the body is unnecessary and inefficient.

   The blocking arm moves along a pendular pathway, makes contact with the inside edge of the Attacker's shin, and then deflects the kick to the side as the arm continues to the final position for a Lower Block.

   d. The Defender does a right Front Snap Kick to the level of the Attacker's belt knot (Fig. 167). (In real situations, the kick would be to the groin or solar plexus.)

Figure 167

   e. After the leg returns to chamber, the right leg steps straight down and the body moves forward with a "heel-toe step" into a right-foot forward upright stance. This stance is like an Itosu Stance, but both feet point directly forward toward the Attacker.

   Note: The "heel-toe step" is done by stepping forward on the heel of the front (right) foot and pulling the back (left) leg forward as the front (right) foot continues forward until the toes touch the ground.

   f. The Defender then "covers" with the left arm by placing the left hand on the Attacker's chest with the fingers extended and pointing along a line that is parallel to the ground. The left arm is bent at the elbow and forms a semicircle (Fig. 168).

Figure 168

g. The left arm stays in the "covering" position as the right hand does a Vertical Punch high (Fig. 169) (Fig. 170).

Note: A Vertical Punch is a punch that does not rotate completely over as the punch is completed. Instead, the rotation stops when the palm is facing sideways (and towards the Center Line) and the knuckles are aligned vertically (Fig. 171).

h. After completing the punch, the Defender recovers by stepping back into Ready Position at the proper starting distance for the Lower Series.

i. Memory aid: The hand that is at chamber is the one that does the Vertical Punch.

Note: If the Attacker's arms were up and in front of the chest in a fighting guard position, the cover would be used to move the arms to the side or temporarily pin them against the Attacker's chest. This cover allows the Defender to feel the movements of the Attacker's arms (and body) and control the arms to prevent another punch. It can also be used to deflect the arms to the side to make room for the punch which follows.

Figure 169

Figure 170

Figure 171

Second Lower Series

1. Attacker

   a. Start in Standard Attacking Position but bring the right hand to chamber position so it does not accidentally get kicked (Fig. 172).

   b. Do a Front Snap Kick with the right leg to the level of the Defender's belt knot. Hold the leg out in its extended position. After the Defender kicks the underside of the extended leg, the Attacker's leg returns to chamber and steps straight down into a Cat Stance (with the kicking leg becoming the front leg of the Cat Stance).

   c. After the Defender completes the series, the leg returns to its original position in Standard Attacking Position.

2. Defender

   a. Start in Ready Position.

   b. Step to the left side into a Cat Stance (with the left leg becoming the back leg of the Cat Stance) to move completely to the outside of the Attacker's kick. The Defender parries the kick with the left hand as the right hand pulls back to chamber in a fist (palm up when done) (Fig. 173).

   The parry is done by bringing the left arm (with the fingers extended and together) across (moving from left to right) in front of the groin until the outside (little-finger) edge of the hand lightly touches the side of the Attacker's leg. The left arm is almost completely extended, but there is a slight bend at the elbow.

   The purpose of the parry is to make contact with the Attacker's leg in order to gather tactile information about the Attacker. It is also a training method for learning how to catch a kick. The purpose is not to block the Attacker's kick. The block is the step to the side into a Cat Stance.

   c. The Defender does a right Front Snap Kick to the underside of the Attacker's right leg near the hip (Fig. 174). (In real situations the kick would be to the inside of the thigh of the supporting leg, the knee of the supporting leg or the groin, with the toes pulled back.)

Figure 172

Figure 173

Figure 174

d. After the leg returns to chamber, the right leg steps straight down and the body moves forward with a "heel-toe step" into a right-foot forward upright stance. This stance is like an Itosu Stance, but both feet point directly forward toward the Attacker.

Note: The "heel-toe step" is done by stepping forward on the heel of the front (right) foot and pulling the back (left) leg forward as the front (right) foot continues forward until the toes touch the ground.

e. The Defender then "covers" with the left arm by placing the left hand on the Attacker's chest (or upper arm) with the fingers extended and pointing along a line that is parallel to the ground. The left arm is bent at the elbow and forms a semicircle.

f. The left arm stays in the "covering" position as the right hand does a Vertical Punch high (Fig. 175).

g. After completing the punch, the Defender recovers by moving back into Ready Position at the proper starting distance for the Lower Series.

h. Memory aid: The hand that is at chamber is the one that does the Vertical Punch.

Figure 175

Third Lower Series

1. Attacker

   a. Start in Standard Attacking Position.

   b. Do a Front Snap Kick with the right leg to the level of the Defender's belt knot. After the kick, the Attacker's leg returns to chamber and steps straight down into a Cat Stance (with the kicking leg becoming the front leg of the Cat Stance).

   c. After the Defender completes the series, the leg returns to its original position in Right Leg Attacking Position.

2. Defender

   a. Start in Ready Position.

   b. Push off the right leg and turn 90 degrees counter-clockwise to the left (pivoting on the heel of the right foot) into a left-foot forward Front Stance to move to the outside of the Attacker's kick. This step is the block for the kick. The step is the same as the first step of the *Taikyuku kata* (described in Chapter XII) except the knees do not bend to start the movement. The movement begins by pushing off the right leg.

   c. The right arm (with the fingers extended and the wrist pulled back as much as possible) bends inward (and the right hand moves upward) until the right thumb is close to the right shoulder with the palm of the hand facing up. The right hand then moves downward along a circular (counterclockwise) pathway until the right hand (with the wrist still pulled back) is one fist away from the front of the right hip and the edge of the forearm is even with the right side of the body. The left hand pulls back to chamber (palm up when done) as the right arm does the preceding move (Fig. 176).

   Key Points: The purpose of this technique with the right arm is to block the kick if it was off to the left side (from the Defender's perspective) of the Defender's Center Line. If it is necessary to use this technique to block the Attacker's kick, then once the right arm has deflected the kick past the Defender's body (which will occur when the right arm is even with the right side of the body), any further movement of the right arm past the right side of the body is unnecessary and inefficient.

Figure 176

Figure 177

If the Attacker has attacked properly (i.e. by kicking directly down the Defender's Center Line), then the move to the outside into a Front Stance will be sufficient to avoid or "block" the kick (Fig. 177 see previous page).

It is important that the right arm does not extend beyond the right side of the body (Fig. 178).

d. The Defender then pushes off the left leg and moves diagonally forward with a "heel-toe step" into a right foot forward upright stance. This stance is like an Itosu Stance, but both feet point directly forward toward the Attacker.

Note: The "heel-toe step" is done by stepping forward on the heel of the front (right) foot and pulling the back (left) leg forward as the front (right) foot continues forward until the toes touch the ground.

Figure 178

e. The Defender then "covers" with the right arm by placing the right hand on the Attacker's chest (or upper arm) with the fingers extended and pointing along a line that is parallel to the ground. The right arm is bent at the elbow and forms a semicircle.

f. The right arm stays in the "covering" position as the left hand does a Vertical Punch high (Fig. 179).

g. After completing the punch, the Defender recovers by moving back into Ready Position at the proper starting distance for the Lower Series.

h. Memory aid: The hand that is at chamber is the one that does the Vertical Punch.

Figure 179

Lower Series — Left Side Series

The Series are identical to the ones listed above except they are done with the opposite side of the body.

XI. Kata

Introduction and General Principles

The practice of *kata* is the culmination of a practitioner's individual training. A significant advantage of *kata* is that techniques can be practiced full force without the risk of injuring partners. *Kata* practice also develops fighting spirit and fighting rhythms. It simulates an actual fighting situation because it allows the practitioner to feel and experience the coordinated movements at full speed and full power without having to "pull" the technique to avoid injuring one's partner. There are many techniques in *kata* that are simply too dangerous to practice with another person. Another advantage is that one can practice *kata* alone when partners are not available.

A key principle when performing *kata* is to imagine that one is actually fighting one or more opponents as the *kata* is executed. This visualization transforms the *kata* from a series of strictly mechanical movements into a meaningful and realistic training aid. One of the highest compliments one can receive after performing a *kata* is that it looked like an actual fight. This is the goal to strive for in *kata* practice.

When done correctly, *kata* practice also teaches the development of a clear mind. At the highest levels of execution, practitioners often feel that their bodies are performing the *kata* without the direction or interference of the conscious mind. The *kata* is simply expressed through them. This mental state is referred to as *mushin* or "no mind."

In an actual encounter, *mushin* is the mental state the practitioner strives to maintain because it enables the practitioner to respond instinctively without the delay or interference of conscious thought. Not only is this type of response quicker, it is also more effective because it draws on the intuitive knowledge of the entire being. This response without conscious thought is the realization of body knowledge. *Kata* practice teaches the practitioner how to enter into this mental state at will, thereby enhancing the practitioner's ability to do this in an actual encounter. This is one of the reasons why traditional Okinawan Karate-do teachers have always emphasized *kata* practice.

In order to get more benefit from the practice of *kata*, one should work separately on "The Seven Ways to Practice *Kata*." The Seven Ways are Form, Power, Speed, Eye Contact, Breathing, Fighting Rhythms, and *Kiai*. Each of these will improve one's ability to execute the techniques in the kata in the most effective manner. By focusing on only one Way at a time, one will improve more quickly than if one is trying to concentrate on a number of Ways at the same time. As each of the different Ways is isolated and improved, a natural integration occurs creating a synergistic effect which makes the techniques substantially more effective.

The Seven Ways to Practice Kata

1. Form

   a. Form is the first Way that one learns and is the most important. If one executes techniques with correct form, one is doing them in the strongest and most efficient (and therefore quickest) manner. Form is something that one is continually refining and perfecting. One never masters a particular technique. Rather, one continually improves and moves closer to perfection.

   b. Poor form causes a "corruption" of the principles. When one corrupts a principle, one loses power and effectiveness proportionately. For example, if one's elbow is not behind the fist when punching (and the elbow is allowed to flare out), one will lose power and strength. For every incremental degree that the elbow moves out to the side when punching, one loses more and more power. This is true for all the principles and is why one must continually strive to execute techniques with the correct form.

c. To improve form, practice the *kata* very slowly and concentrate on doing each technique with the proper checkpoints and correct application of principles. At the same time, visualize yourself doing the technique perfectly.

2. Power

a. One key to increasing power is to utilize more of the body. The legs, hips, shoulders, and arms (for punches) must work together to produce the maximum amount of force. The correct timing and sequence of the motions comprising the techniques are critical.

b. To improve power, concentrate on doing each technique as forcefully as possible with the correct sequence of body parts. It helps to pause slightly between each technique because this allows time to concentrate on generating the greatest amount of power.

3. Speed

a. Relaxation equals speed. One of the biggest barriers to increasing speed is excessive (and unnecessary) tension in the muscles. Unfortunately, tension often increases when one tries to do a motion faster. This is because the "trying" gets in the way of the "doing." Less effort is better than more effort when it comes to increasing speed.

b. To improve speed, concentrate on staying loose and relaxed while avoiding trying too hard. Do not worry about the amount of force generated by the techniques. The techniques should be light and quick when practiced for speed.

4. Eye Contact

a. Eye contact emphasizes the visualization of opponents as the *kata* is executed. Without this visualization, *kata* practice cannot simulate the feeling of an actual fight and practice will not be as beneficial as it could be.

b. To improve and practice eye contact, look sharply on each turn and actually "see" an opponent in the mind's eye. Try to feel each block deflecting an attack and each strike making contact with an opponent.

5. Breathing

a. The goal is to coordinate breathing from the diaphragm with the execution of techniques. This helps to control one's respiration rate and may be used to augment power. To breathe from the diaphragm when inhaling, the lower belly (and not the chest) should expand first as air is brought into the lungs. To breathe from the diaphragm when exhaling, the lower belly should pull inward to force the air out of the lungs.

b. To practice coordinating breathing with the execution of techniques, inhale on blocking techniques and exhale on striking techniques. The exhales should be short, focused, bursts of air done with the teeth together. This is sometimes described as "spitting" out the air.

6. Fighting Rhythms

a. The timing and rhythm of attacks and counters in an actual fight is erratic. It is therefore important to train oneself to adjust to varying speeds. All blocking techniques are ineffective if they are done too fast or too slow. The timing needs to match exactly the speed of the attack.

b. To practice *kata* for the development of fighting rhythms, break the *kata* down into series that seem logically connected. Each series should represent an encounter with one or more opponents. Try to simulate the rhythm of an actual fight by varying the speed and pausing between each series. If *kata* is not practiced for Fighting Rhythms, the *kata* may become a purely mechanical repetition of choreographed movements.

7. *Kiai*

a. *Kiai* means to unite the spirit or internal energies. The idea is to coordinate all of the entire being's energy into the execution of the techniques. A *kiai* is frequently done by forcing the air out of the diaphragm while executing a punch or kick. The forced exhale is what produces the loud shout one normally associates with a *kiai*.

b. When done properly, a *kiai* unites one's internal energies with the physical energy produced by the contraction of the muscle. This makes the techniques incredibly powerful.

c. To practice with *kiai*, imagine all of the energy of the entire being is unified and projected outward as the technique is executed. There should be a feeling of intense focus. It helps to add the loud shout to some of the punches, kicks, or strikes in the kata.

Key Points and Principles for All the Taikyuku Kata

1. Look before starting each turn. The look is done by quickly rotating the head so that the eyes are looking in the direction the body will be facing after completion of the turn.

2. All turns pivot on the heel (not the ball) of the foot that becomes the back foot of the completed Front Stance and pivot on the ball of the foot that becomes the front foot of the completed Front Stance.

3. Once the knees are bent to start the first turn, the body should not rise up or drop down as subsequent steps and turns are done. The head should remain at the same height throughout the entire kata. This enables the maximum amount of power to be derived from the steps and turns. In addition, if the body rises up or drops down when moving, this will "telegraph" the punch (or kick) and will reduce the amount of power transferred from the legs to the arms.

4. There should be a feeling of driving and pushing off the back leg as a turn is completed. The power from the back leg is continued and augmented by the rotation of the hips. These motions generate and transfer power and momentum from the legs into the upper body and arms. The power from the legs is transferred to the blocking arm on the turn by starting the block just before the turn is completed. This transfer of power from the legs and hips to the upper body and arms is a key aspect of the *Taikyuku Kata*.

5. When circle stepping forward, the punch starts just as the front foot stops and the knee starts to move forward over the toes. This timing of the punch ensures that the body is grounded or stable when the punch makes contact with an opponent. It also transfers the momentum and power of the body's forward motion into the punch. This timing is the key principle for punches in both the *Kiyan* lines and the *Taiyuku Kata*.

6. The footwork pattern and stepping for *Taikyuku Shodan*, *Taikyuku Nidan* and *Taikyuku Sandan* are identical. The only differences are the blocks, punches and kicks used after completion of the turns and steps. The first section of the *Taikyuku Kata* Chapter shows the footwork pattern and stepping without any hand or leg techniques to make it easier to learn.

XII. Taikyuku Kata

Stepping for the Taikyuku Kata

1. Opening: Start in Informal Attention Stance (*Musubi Dachi*) (Fig. 180). Bow. Step out into Ready Position (Fig. 181).

2. 90 Degree Turn and Side Series:

   a. Look to the left.

   b. Bend both knees and shift the weight to the right leg, then put the left foot out to the left side and to the left of (behind) an imaginary line drawn parallel to the shoulders at the back of the right heel (Fig. 182) (Fig. 183).

   c. Turn 90 degrees counterclockwise to the left (pivoting on the heel of the right foot and the ball of the left foot) into a left-foot forward Front Stance (*Zen Kutsu Dachi*) (Fig. 184).

   d. Circle step forward into a right-foot forward Front Stance (Fig. 185).

(See pages 150-152 for a complete stepping chart.)

Figure 180

Figure 181

Figure 182

Figure 183 Side View

Figure 184

Figure 185

3. 180 Degree Turn and Side Series:

a. Look behind by looking over the right shoulder.

b. Shift the weight to the left leg without rising up, then put the right foot diagonally behind and to the left of (across) the left leg (Fig. 186) (Fig. 187).

c. Turn 180 degrees clockwise to the right (pivoting on the heel of the left foot and the ball of the right foot) into a right-foot forward Front Stance (Fig. 188) (Fig. 189).

d. Circle step forward into a left-foot forward Front Stance (Fig. 190).

Figure 186

Figure 187 Side View

Figure 188

Figure 189 Side View

Figure 190

4. 90 Degree Turn and Down Center Series:

a. Look to the left.

b. Shift the weight to the right leg without rising up (Fig. 191), then put the left foot out to the left side and to the left of (behind) an imaginary line drawn parallel to the shoulders at the back of the heel of the right foot (Fig. 192).

c. Turn 90 degrees counterclockwise to the left (pivoting on the heel of the right foot and the ball of the left foot) into a left-foot forward Front Stance (Fig. 193).

d. Circle step forward into a right-foot forward Front Stance (Fig. 194).

e. Circle step forward into a left-foot forward Front Stance (Fig. 195).

f. Circle step forward into a right-foot forward Front Stance (Fig. 196).

Figure 191

Figure 192

Figure 193

Figure 194

Figure 195

Figure 196

5. 270 Degree Turn and Side Series:

a. Look 270 degrees to the left by turning the head and upper body counterclockwise as much as possible.

b. Turn the right foot in toward the center of the body (pivoting on the heel) (Fig. 197), shift the weight to the right leg without rising up, and then bring the left foot diagonally forward and across (behind) the back of the right leg to a position that is at approximately 2 o'clock with respect to the right foot (Fig. 198) (Fig. 199).

c. Turn 270 degrees counterclockwise to the left (pivoting on the heel of the right foot and the ball of the left foot) into a left-foot forward Front Stance (Fig. 200).

d. Circle step forward into a right-foot forward Front Stance (Fig. 201).

Figure 197

Figure 198

Figure 199 - Side View

Figure 200

Figure 201

6. 180 Degree Turn and Side Series:

   a. Look behind by looking over the right shoulder.

   b. Shift the weight to the left leg without rising up, then put the right foot diagonally behind and to the left of (across) the left leg (Fig. 202).

   c. Turn 180 degrees clockwise to the right (pivoting on the heel of the left foot and the ball of the right foot) into a right-foot forward Front Stance (Fig. 203).

   d. Circle step forward into a left-foot forward Front Stance (Fig. 204).

Figure 202

Figure 203

Figure 204

7. 90 Degree Turn and Down Center Series:

a. Look to the left.

b. Shift the weight to the right leg without rising up (Fig. 205), then put the left foot out to the left side and to the left of (behind) an imaginary line drawn parallel to the shoulders at the back of the heel of the right foot (Fig. 206).

c. Turn 90 degrees counterclockwise to the left (pivoting on the heel of the right foot and the ball of the left foot) into a left-foot forward Front Stance (Fig. 207).

d. Circle step forward into a right-foot forward Front Stance (Fig. 208).

e. Circle step forward into a left-foot forward Front Stance (Fig. 209).

f. Circle step forward into a right-foot forward Front Stance (Fig. 210).

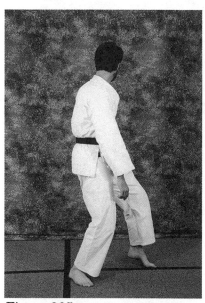

Figure 205

Figure 206

Figure 207

Figure 208

Figure 209

Figure 210

8. 270 Degree Turn and Side Series:

a. Look 270 degrees to the left by turning the head and upper body counterclockwise as much as possible.

b. Turn the right foot in toward the center of the body (pivoting on the heel) (Fig. 211), shift the weight to the right leg without rising up, and then bring the left foot diagonally forward and across (behind) the back of the right leg to a position that is at approximately 2 o'clock with respect to the right foot (Fig. 212).

c. Turn 270 degrees counterclockwise to the left (pivoting on the heel of the right foot and the ball of the left foot) into a left-foot forward Front Stance (Fig. 213).

d. Circle step forward into a right-foot forward Front Stance (Fig. 214).

Figure 211

Figure 212

Figure 213

Figure 214

9. 180 Degree Turn and Side Series:

  a. Look behind by looking over the right shoulder.

  b. Shift the weight to the left leg without rising up, then put the right foot diagonally behind and to the left of (across) the left leg (Fig. 215).

  c. Turn 180 degrees clockwise to the right (pivoting on the heel of the left foot and the ball of the right foot) into a right-foot forward Front Stance (Fig. 216).

  d. Circle step forward into a left-foot forward Front Stance (Fig. 217).

Figure 215

Figure 216

Figure 217

10. Recovery — *No-te*

a. Recover by pushing off the left foot and turning 90 degrees counterclockwise to the left and then pushing off the right foot until the body faces the original direction with the feet slightly wider than shoulder width apart.

b. The knees should still be bent and the eyes look to the right (the direction previously faced) the entire time.

c. The arms come to Ready Position (Fig. 218).

d. Stand up slowly while still looking to the right (Fig. 219), then look directly forward (i.e. the direction the body is facing) (Fig. 220).

e. Bring the left foot next to the right foot and bring the arms to the sides of the body (Fig. 221).

f. The Taikyuku kata is completed with a bow.

11. Key Points:

a. Look before starting each turn.

b. All turns pivot on the heel (not the ball) of the back foot.

c. The body should not rise up or drop down during the kata.

d. There should be a feeling of driving and pushing off the back leg as a turn is done.

Figure 218

Figure 219

Figure 220

Figure 221

Stepping Chart for all Taikyuku Kata

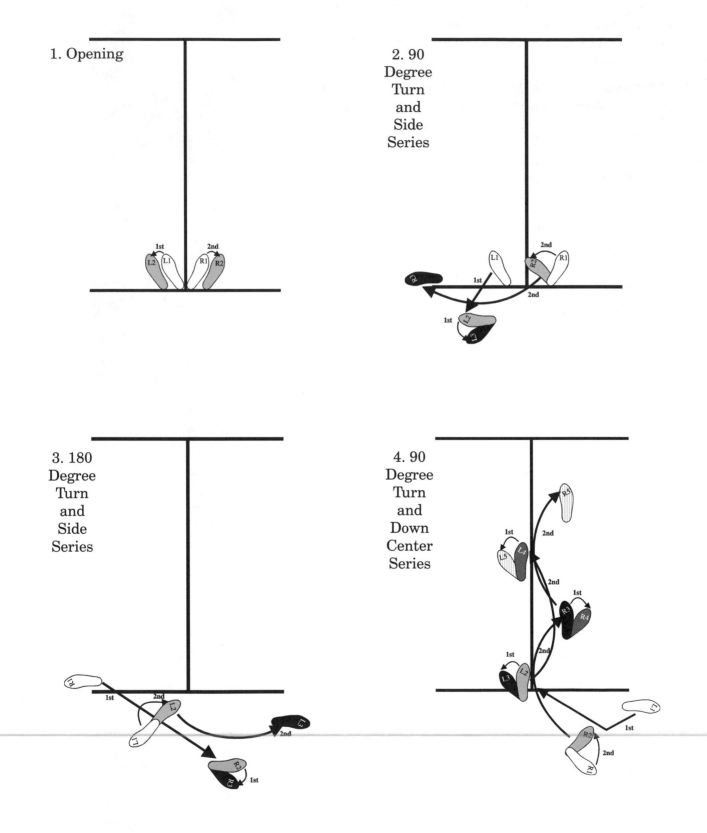

1. Opening

2. 90 Degree Turn and Side Series

3. 180 Degree Turn and Side Series

4. 90 Degree Turn and Down Center Series

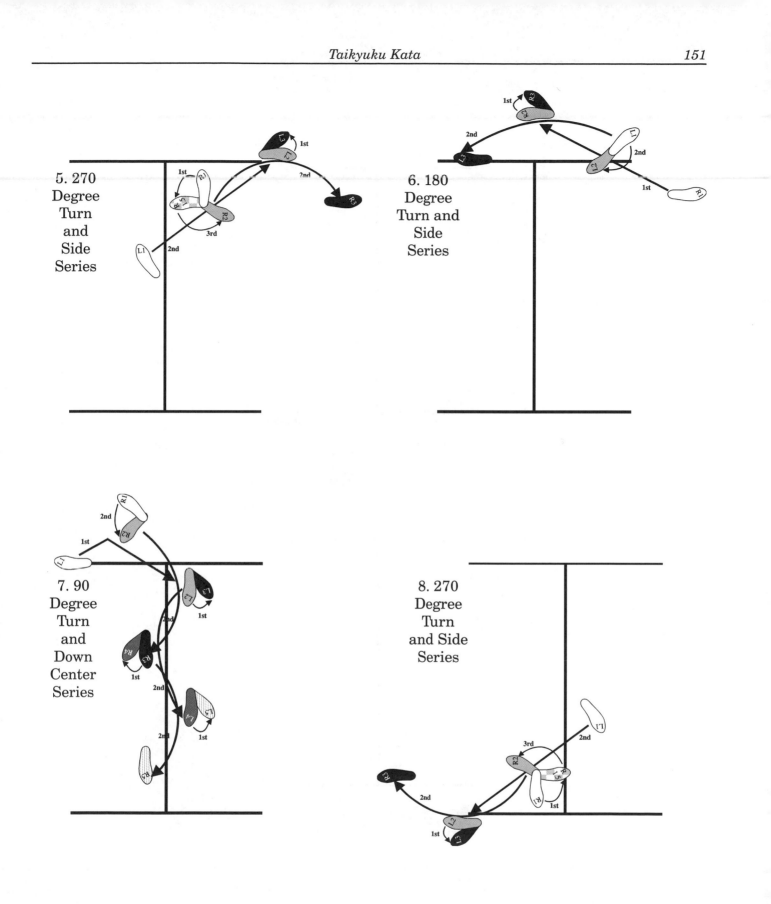

5. 270 Degree Turn and Side Series

6. 180 Degree Turn and Side Series

7. 90 Degree Turn and Down Center Series

8. 270 Degree Turn and Side Series

9. 180 Degree Turn and Side Series

10. Recovery (*No-te*)

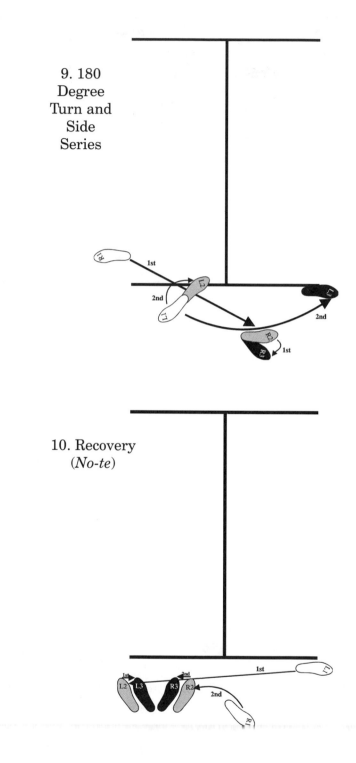

Taikyuku Shodan

1. Opening: Start in Informal Attention Stance (*Musubi Dachi*) (Fig. 222). Bow. Step out into Ready Position (Fig. 223).

2. 90 Degree Turn and Side Series:

   a. Look to the left.

   b. Bend both knees and shift the weight to the right leg, then put the left foot out to the left side and to the left of (behind) an imaginary line drawn parallel to the shoulders at the back of the right heel.

   c. Turn 90 degrees counterclockwise to the left (pivoting on the heel of the right foot and the ball of the left foot) into a left-foot forward Front Stance and do a Lower Block with the left arm as the right hand pulls simultaneously back to chamber (palm up when done) (Fig. 224).

   d. Circle step forward into a right-foot forward Front Stance and do a right Lunge Punch middle (palm down when done) as the left hand pulls back to chamber (palm up when done) (Fig. 225).

Figure 222

Figure 223

Figure 224

Figure 225

3. 180 Degree Turn and Side Series:

   a. Look behind by looking over the right shoulder.

   b. Shift the weight to the left leg without rising up, then put the right foot diagonally behind and to the left of (across) the left leg.

   c. Turn 180 degrees clockwise to the right (pivoting on the heel of the left foot and the ball of the right foot) into a right-foot forward Front Stance and do a Lower Block with the right arm as the left hand simultaneously pulls back to chamber (palm up when done) (Fig. 226).

   d. Circle step forward into a left-foot forward Front Stance and do a left Lunge Punch middle (palm down when done) as the right hand simultaneously pulls back to chamber (palm up when done) (Fig. 227).

Figure 226

Figure 227

4. 90 Degree Turn and Down Center Series:

a. Look to the left.

b. Shift the weight to the right leg without rising up, then put the left foot out to the left side and to the left of (behind) an imaginary line drawn parallel to the shoulders at the back of the heel of the right foot.

Figure 228

c. Turn 90 degrees counterclockwise to the left (pivoting on the heel of the right foot and the ball of the left foot) into a left-foot forward Front Stance and do a Lower Block with the left arm as the right hand simultaneously pulls back to chamber (palm up when done) (Fig. 228).

d. Circle step forward into a right-foot forward Front Stance and do a right Lunge Punch middle (palm down when done) as the left hand simultaneously pulls back to chamber (palm up when done) (Fig. 229).

Figure 229

e. Circle step forward into a left-foot forward Front Stance and do a left Lunge Punch middle (palm down when done) as the right hand simultaneously pulls back to chamber (palm up when done) (Fig. 230).

f. Circle step forward into a right-foot forward Front Stance and do a right Lunge Punch middle (palm down when done) as the left hand simultaneously pulls back to chamber (palm up when done) (Fig. 231). *Kiai* on the punch.

Figure 230

A *kiai* is a loud sound caused by contracting the diaphragm to force air out of the mouth. It is used to increase the power of the technique (augmentation with breath power), to contract the stomach muscles in case of a counterattack, and to startle and freeze an opponent.

Figure 231

5. 270 Degree Turn and Side Series:

   a. Look 270 degrees to the left by turning the head and upper body counterclockwise as much as possible.

   b. Turn the right foot in toward the center of the body (pivoting on the heel), shift the weight to the right leg without rising up, and then bring the left foot diagonally forward and across (behind) the back of the right leg to a position that is at approximately 2 o'clock with respect to the right foot.

   c. Turn 270 degrees counterclockwise to the left (pivoting on the heel of the right foot and the ball of the left foot) into a left-foot forward Front Stance and do a Lower Block with the left arm as the right hand simultaneously pulls back to chamber (palm up when done) (Fig. 232).

   d. Circle step forward into a right-foot forward Front Stance and do a right Lunge Punch middle (palm down when done) as the left hand simultaneously pulls back to chamber (palm up when done) (Fig. 233).

Figure 232

Figure 233

6. 180 Degree Turn and Side Series:

   a. Look behind by looking over the right shoulder.

   b. Shift the weight to the left leg without rising up, then put the right foot diagonally behind and to the left of (across) the left leg.

   c. Turn 180 degrees clockwise to the right (pivoting on the heel of the left foot and the ball of the right foot) into a right-foot forward Front Stance and do a Lower Block with the right arm as the left hand simultaneously pulls back to chamber (palm up when done) (Fig. 234).

   d. Circle step forward into a left-foot forward Front Stance and do a left Lunge Punch middle (palm down when done) as the right hand simultaneously pulls back to chamber (palm up when done) (Fig. 235).

Figure 234

Figure 235

7. 90 Degree Turn and Down Center Series:

a. Look to the left.

b. Shift the weight to the right leg without rising up, then put the left foot out to the left side and to the left of (behind) an imaginary line drawn parallel to the shoulders at the back of the heel of the right foot.

c. Turn 90 degrees counterclockwise to the left (pivoting on the heel of the right foot and the ball of the left foot) into a left foot forward Front Stance and do a Lower Block with the left arm as the right hand simultaneously pulls back to chamber (palm up when done) (Fig. 236).

Figure 236

d. Circle step forward into a right-foot forward Front Stance and do a right Lunge Punch middle (palm down when done) as the left hand simultaneously pulls back to chamber (palm up when done) (Fig. 237).

e. Circle step forward into a left-foot forward Front Stance and do a left Lunge Punch middle (palm down when done) as the right hand simultaneously pulls back to chamber (palm up when done) (Fig. 238).

Figure 237

f. Circle step forward into a right-foot forward Front Stance and do a right Lunge Punch middle (palm down when done) as the left hand simultaneously pulls back to chamber (palm up when done) (Fig. 239). *Kiai* on the punch.

Figure 238

Figure 239

8. 270 Degree Turn and Side Series:

a. Look 270 degrees to the left by turning the head and upper body counterclockwise as much as possible.

b. Turn the right foot in toward the center of the body (pivoting on the heel), shift the weight to the right leg without rising up, and then bring the left foot diagonally forward and across (behind) the back of the right leg to a position that is at approximately 2 o'clock with respect to the right foot.

c. Turn 270 degrees counterclockwise to the left (pivoting on the heel of the right foot and the ball of the left foot) into a left-foot forward Front Stance and do a Lower Block with the left arm as the right hand simultaneously pulls back to chamber (palm up when done) (Fig. 240).

d. Circle step forward into a right-foot forward Front Stance and do a right Lunge Punch middle (palm down when done) as the left hand simultaneously pulls back to chamber (palm up when done) (Fig. 241).

Figure 240

Figure 241

9. 180 Degree Turn and Side Series:

   a. Look behind by looking over the right shoulder.

   b. Shift the weight to the left leg without rising up, then put the right foot diagonally behind and to the left of (across) the left leg.

   c. Turn 180 degrees clockwise to the right (pivoting on the heel of the left foot and the ball of the right foot) into a right-foot forward Front Stance and do a Lower Block with the right arm as the left hand simultaneously pulls back to chamber (palm up when done) (Fig. 242).

   d. Circle step forward into a left-foot forward Front Stance and do a left Lunge Punch middle (palm down when done) as the right hand simultaneously pulls back to chamber (palm up when done) (Fig. 243).

Figure 242

Figure 243

10. Recovery — *No-te*

a. Recover by pushing off the left foot and turning 90 degrees counterclockwise to the left and then pushing off the right foot until the body faces the original direction with the feet slightly wider than shoulder width apart.

b. The knees should still be bent and the eyes look to the right (the direction previously faced) the entire time.

c. The arms come to Ready Position (Fig. 244).

d. Stand up slowly while still looking to the right, then look directly forward (i.e. the direction the body is facing) (Fig. 245).

e. Bring the left foot next to the right foot and bring the arms to the sides of the body (Fig. 246).

f. The *Taikyuku kata* is completed with a bow.

Figure 244

Figure 245

Figure 246

Memory Aids

1. There is a Lower Block on every turn.

2. The Lower Block is done with the arm that is on the same side of the body as the shoulder that you are looking over before the turn is started.

   If the head is turned counterclockwise and the "look" before the turn is started is over the left shoulder, then the Lower Block will be done with the left arm.

   If the head is turned clockwise and the "look" before the turn is started is over the right shoulder, then the Lower Block will be done with the right arm.

3. Every punch is a middle Lunge Punch with the arm that is on the same side of the body as the front leg of the Front Stance.

4. *Kiai* on the third punch of the 90 Degree Turn and Down Center Series.

Taikyuku Nidan

1. Opening: Start in Informal Attention Stance (*Musubi Dachi*) (Fig. 247). Bow. Step out into Ready Position (Fig. 248).

2. 90 Degree Turn and Side Series:

   a. Look to the left.

   b. Bend both knees and shift the weight to the right leg, then put the left foot out to the left side and to the left of (behind) an imaginary line drawn parallel to the shoulders at the back of the right heel.

   c. Turn 90 degrees counterclockwise to the left (pivoting on the heel of the right foot and the ball of the left foot) into a left-foot forward Front Stance and do a Middle Block with the left arm as the right hand simultaneously pulls back to chamber (palm up when done) (Fig. 249).

   d. Circle step forward into a right-foot forward Front Stance and do a right Upper Block as the left hand simultaneously pulls back to chamber (palm up when done) (Fig. 250).

   e. Do a left Reverse Punch middle (palm down when done) as the right hand simultaneously pulls back to chamber (palm up when done) (Fig. 251).

Figure 247

Figure 248

Figure 249

Figure 250

Figure 251

3. 180 Degree Turn and Side Series:

    a. Look behind by looking over the right shoulder.

    b. Shift the weight to the left leg without rising up, then put the right foot diagonally behind and to the left of (across) the left leg.

    c. Turn 180 degrees clockwise to the right (pivoting on the heel of the left foot and the ball of the right foot) into a right-foot forward Front Stance and do a Middle Block with the right arm as the left hand pulls back to chamber (palm up when done) (Fig. 252).

    d. Circle step forward into a left-foot forward Front Stance and do a left Upper Block as the right hand simultaneously pulls back to chamber (palm up when done) (Fig. 253).

    e. Do a right Reverse Punch middle (palm down when done) as the left hand simultaneously pulls back to chamber (palm up when done) (Fig. 254).

Figure 252

Figure 253

Figure 254

4. 90 Degree Turn and Down Center Series:

a. Look to the left.

b. Shift the weight to the right leg without rising up, then put the left foot out to the left side and to the left of (behind) an imaginary line drawn parallel to the shoulders at the back of the heel of the right foot.

c. Turn 90 degrees counterclockwise to the left (pivoting on the heel of the right foot and the ball of the left foot) into a left foot forward Front Stance and do a Lower Block with the left arm as the right hand pulls back to chamber (palm up when done) (Fig. 255).

d. Do a right Reverse Punch middle (palm down when done) as the left hand pulls back to chamber (palm up when done) (Fig. 256).

e. Circle step forward into a right foot forward Front Stance and do a left Reverse Punch middle (palm down when done) as the right hand pulls back to chamber (palm up when donc) (Fig. 257).

f. Circle step forward into a left foot forward Front Stance and do a right Reverse Punch middle (palm down when done) as the left hand pulls back to chamber (palm up when done) (Fig. 258).

g. Circle step forward into a right-foot forward Front Stance and do a left Reverse Punch middle (palm down when done) as the right hand pulls back to chamber (palm up when done) (Fig. 259). *Kiai* on the punch.

Figure 255

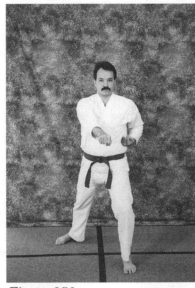
Figure 256

Figure 257

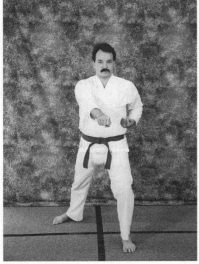
Figure 258

Figure 259

5. 270 Degree Turn and Side Series:

   a. Look 270 degrees to the left by turning the head and upper body counterclockwise as much as possible.

   b. Turn the right foot in toward the center of the body (pivoting on the heel), shift the weight to the right leg without rising up, and then bring the left foot diagonally forward and across (behind) the back of the right leg to a position that is at approximately 2 o'clock with respect to the right foot.

   c. Turn 270 degrees counterclockwise to the left (pivoting on the heel of the right foot and the ball of the left foot) into a left-foot forward Front Stance and do a Middle Block with the left arm as the right hand simultaneously pulls back to chamber (palm up when done) (Fig. 260).

Figure 260

   d. Circle step forward into a right-foot forward Front Stance and do a right Upper Block as the left hand simultaneously pulls back to chamber (palm up when done) (Fig. 261).

   e. Do a left Reverse Punch middle (palm down when done) as the right hand simultaneously pulls back to chamber (palm up when done) (Fig. 262).

Figure 261

Figure 262

6. 180 Degree Turn and Side Series:

   a. Look behind by looking over the right shoulder.

   b. Shift the weight to the left leg without rising up, then put the right foot diagonally behind and to the left of (across) the left leg.

   c. Turn 180 degrees clockwise to the right (pivoting on the heel of the left foot and the ball of the right foot) into a right-foot forward Front Stance and do a Middle Block with the right arm as the left hand simultaneously pulls back to chamber (palm up when done) (Fig. 263).

Figure 263

   d. Circle step forward into a left-foot forward Front Stance and do a left Upper Block as the right hand simultaneously pulls back to chamber (palm up when done) (Fig. 264).

   e. Do a right Reverse Punch middle (palm down when done) as the left hand simultaneously pulls back to chamber (palm up when done) (Fig. 265).

Figure 264

Figure 265

7. 90 Degree Turn and Down Center Series:

a. Look to the left.

b. Shift the weight to the right leg without rising up, then put the left foot out to the left side and to the left of (behind) an imaginary line drawn parallel to the shoulders at the back of the heel of the right foot.

c. Turn 90 degrees counterclockwise to the left (pivoting on the heel of the right foot and the ball of the left foot) into a left-foot forward Front Stance and do a Lower Block with the left arm as the right hand pulls back to chamber (palm up when done) (Fig. 266).

d. Do a right Reverse Punch middle (palm down when done) as the left hand pulls back to chamber (palm up when done) (Fig. 267).

e. Circle step forward into a right foot forward Front Stance and do a left Reverse Punch middle (palm down when done) as the right hand pulls back to chamber (palm up when done) (Fig. 268).

f. Circle step forward into a left foot forward Front Stance and do a right Reverse Punch middle (palm down when done) as the left hand pulls back to chamber (palm up when done) (Fig. 269).

g. Circle step forward into a right foot forward Front Stance and do a left Reverse Punch middle (palm down when done) as the right hand pulls back to chamber (palm up when done) (Fig. 270). *Kiai* on the punch.

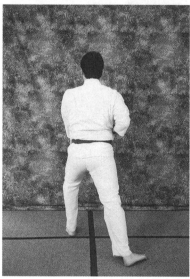

Figure 266

Figure 267

Figure 268

Figure 269

Figure 270

8. 270 Degree Turn and Side Series:

a. Look 270 degrees to the left by turning the head and upper body counterclockwise as much as possible.

b. Turn the right foot in toward the center of the body (pivoting on the heel), shift the weight to the right leg without rising up, and then bring the left foot diagonally forward and across (behind) the back of the right leg to a position that is at approximately 2 o'clock with respect to the right foot.

c. Turn 270 degrees counterclockwise to the left (pivoting on the heel of the right foot and the ball of the left foot) into a left-foot forward Front Stance and do a Middle Block with the left arm as the right hand simultaneously pulls back to chamber (palm up when done) (Fig. 271).

d. Circle step forward into a right-foot forward Front Stance and do a right Upper Block as the left hand simultaneously pulls back to chamber (palm up when done) (Fig. 272).

e. Do a left Reverse Punch middle (palm down when done) as the right hand simultaneously pulls back to chamber (palm up when done) (Fig. 273).

Figure 271

Figure 272

Figure 273

9. 180 Degree Turn and Side Series:

a. Look behind by looking over the right shoulder.

b. Shift the weight to the left leg without rising up, then put the right foot diagonally behind and to the left of (across) the left leg.

c. Turn 180 degrees clockwise to the right (pivoting on the heel of the left foot and the ball of the right foot) into a right-foot forward Front Stance and do a Middle Block with the right arm as the left hand simultaneously pulls back to chamber (palm up when done) (Fig. 274).

d. Circle step forward into a left-foot forward Front Stance and do a left Upper Block as the right hand simultaneously pulls back to chamber (palm up when done) (Fig. 275).

e. Do a right Reverse Punch middle (palm down when done) as the left hand simultaneously pulls back to chamber (palm up when done) (Fig. 276).

Figure 274

Figure 275

Figure 276

10. Recovery — *No-te*

a. Recover by pushing off the left foot as the body begins to turn 90 degrees counterclockwise to the left and then pushing off the right foot until the body completes the turn and faces the original direction with the feet slightly wider than shoulder width apart.

b. The knees should still be bent and the eyes look to the right (the direction previously faced) the entire time.

c. The arms come to Ready Position (Fig. 277).

d. Stand up slowly while still looking to the right, then look directly forward (i.e. the direction the body is facing) (Fig. 278).

e. Bring the left foot next to the right foot and bring the arms to the sides of the body (Fig. 279).

f. The *Taikyuku kata* is completed with a bow.

Figure 277

Figure 278

Figure 279

Memory Aids

1. The Middle Block or Lower Block on the turns is done with the arm that is on the same side of the body as the shoulder that you are looking over before the turn is started.

   a. If the head is turned counterclockwise and the "look" before the turn is over the left shoulder, then the Middle Block or Lower Block will be done with the left arm.

   b. If the head is turned clockwise and the "look" before the turn is over the right shoulder, then the Middle Block or Lower Block will be done with the right arm.

2. Every punch is a middle Reverse Punch with the arm that is on the same side of the body as the back leg of the Front Stance.

3. *Kiai* on the punch on the third step of the 90 Degree Turn and Down Center Series.

Taikyuku Sandan

1. Opening: Start in Informal Attention Stance (*Musubi Dachi*) (Fig. 280). Bow. Step out into Ready Position (Fig. 281).

2. 90 Degree Turn and Side Series:

   a. Look to the left.

   b. Bend both knees and shift the weight to the right leg, then put the left foot out to the left side and to the left of (behind) an imaginary line drawn parallel to the shoulders at the back of the right heel.

   c. Turn 90 degrees counterclockwise to the left (pivoting on the heel of the right foot and the ball of the left foot) into a left-foot forward Front Stance and do a Lower Block with the left arm as the right hand pulls back to chamber (palm up when done) (Fig. 282).

   d. Do a Front Snap Kick with the right leg and then return the leg to its starting position in a Front Stance (Fig. 283).

   e. Do a right Reverse Punch middle (palm down when done) as the left hand pulls back to chamber (palm up when done) (Fig. 284).

   f. Circle step forward into a right-foot forward Front Stance and do a left Reverse Punch middle (palm down when done) as the right hand pulls back to chamber (palm up when done) (Fig. 285)

Figure 280

Figure 281

Figure 282

Figure 283

Figure 284

Figure 285

3. 180 Degree Turn and Side Series:

  a. Look behind by looking over the right shoulder.

  b. Shift the weight to the left leg without rising up, then put the right foot diagonally behind and to the left of (across) the left leg.

  c. Turn 180 degrees clockwise to the right (pivoting on the heel of the left foot and the ball of the right foot) into a right-foot forward Front Stance and do a Lower Block with the right arm as the left hand pulls back to chamber (palm up when done) (Fig. 286).

  d. Do a Front Snap Kick with the left leg and then return the leg to its starting position in a Front Stance (Fig. 287).

  e. Do a left Reverse Punch middle (palm down when done) as the right hand pulls back to chamber (palm up when done) (Fig. 288).

  f. Circle step forward into a left-foot forward Front Stance and do a right Reverse Punch middle (palm down when done) as the left hand simultaneously pulls back to chamber (palm up when done) (Fig. 289).

Figure 286

Figure 287

Figure 288

Figure 289

4. 90 Degree Turn and Down Center Series:

a. Look to the left.

b. Shift the weight to the right leg without rising up, then put the left foot out to the left side and to the left of (behind) an imaginary line drawn parallel to the shoulders at the back of the heel of the right foot.

c. Turn 90 degrees counterclockwise to the left (pivoting on the heel of the right foot and the ball of the left foot) into a left-foot forward Front Stance and do a Lower Block with the left arm as the right hand pulls back to chamber (palm up when done) (Fig. 290).

d. Circle step forward into a right-foot forward Front Stance and do a right Lunge Punch high (palm down when done) as the left hand pulls back to chamber (palm up when done) (Fig. 291). Do a left Reverse Punch middle (palm down when done) as the right hand pulls back to chamber (palm up when done) (Fig. 292).

e. Circle step forward into a left-foot forward Front Stance and do a right Reverse Punch high (palm down when done) as the left hand pulls back to chamber (palm up when done) (Fig. 293). Do a left Lunge Punch middle (palm down when done) as the right hand pulls back to chamber (palm up when done) (Fig. 294).

f. Circle step forward into a right-foot forward Front Stance and do a right Lunge Punch high (palm down when done) as the left hand pulls back to chamber (palm up when done) (Fig. 295). Do a left Reverse Punch middle (palm down when done) as the right hand pulls back to chamber (palm up when done) (Fig. 296). *Kiai* on the second punch.

Figure 290

Figure 291

Figure 292

Figure 293

Figure 294

Figure 295

Figure 296

5. 270 Degree Turn and Side Series:

   a. Look 270 degrees to the left by turning the head and upper body counterclockwise as much as possible.

   b. Turn the right foot in toward the center of the body (pivoting on the heel), shift the weight to the right leg without rising up, and then bring the left foot diagonally forward and across (behind) the back of the right leg to a position that is at approximately 2 o'clock with respect to the right foot.

   c. Turn 270 degrees counterclockwise to the left (pivoting on the heel of the right foot and the ball of the left foot) into a left foot forward Front Stance and do a Lower Block with the left arm as the right hand pulls back to chamber (palm up when done) (Fig. 297).

Figure 297

   d. Do a Front Snap Kick with the right leg and then return the leg to its starting position in a Front Stance (Fig. 298).

   e. Do a right Reverse Punch middle (palm down when done) as the left hand simultaneously pulls back to chamber (palm up when done) (Fig. 299).

   f. Circle step forward into a right foot forward Front Stance and do a left Reverse Punch middle (palm down when done) as the right hand simultaneously pulls back to chamber (palm up when done) (Fig. 300).

Figure 298

Figure 299

Figure 300

6. 180 Degree Turn and Side Series:

a. Look behind by looking over the right shoulder.

b. Shift the weight to the left leg without rising up, then put the right foot diagonally behind and to the left of (across) the left leg.

c. Turn 180 degrees clockwise to the right (pivoting on the heel of the left foot and the ball of the right foot) into a right-foot forward Front Stance and do a Lower Block with the right arm as the left hand simultaneously pulls back to chamber (palm up when done) (Fig. 301).

Figure 301

d. Do a Front Snap Kick with the left leg and then return the leg to its starting position in a Front Stance (Fig. 302).

e. Do a left Reverse Punch middle (palm down when done) as the right hand simultaneously pulls back to chamber (palm up when done) (Fig. 303).

Figure 302

f. Circle step forward into a left-foot forward Front Stance and do a right Reverse Punch middle (palm down when done) as the left hand simultaneously pulls back to chamber (palm up when done) (Fig. 304).

Figure 303

Figure 304

7. 90 Degree Turn and Down Center Series:

a. Look to the left.

b. Shift the weight to the right leg without rising up, then put the left foot out to the left side and to the left of (behind) an imaginary line drawn parallel to the shoulders at the back of the heel of the right foot.

c. Turn 90 degrees counterclockwise to the left (pivoting on the heel of the right foot and the ball of the left foot) into a left foot forward Front Stance and do a Lower Block with the left arm as the right hand pulls back to chamber (palm up when done) (Fig. 305).

d. Circle step forward into a right foot forward Front Stance and do a right Lunge Punch high (palm down when done) as the left hand pulls back to chamber (palm up when done) (Fig. 306). Do a left Reverse Punch middle (palm down when done) as the right hand pulls back to chamber (palm up when done) (Fig. 307).

e. Circle step forward into a left foot forward Front Stance and do a right Reverse Punch high (palm down when done) as the left hand pulls back to chamber (palm up when done) (Fig. 308). Do a left Lunge Punch middle (palm down when done) as the right hand pulls back to chamber (palm up when done) (Fig. 309).

f. Circle step forward into a right foot forward Front Stance and do a right Lunge Punch high (palm down whcn done) as the left hand pulls back to chamber (palm up when done) (Fig. 310). Do a left Reverse Punch middle (palm down when done) as the right hand pulls back to chamber (palm up when done) (Fig. 311). *Kiai* on the second punch.

Figure 305

Figure 306

Figure 307

Figure 308

Figure 309

Figure 310

Figure 311

8. 270 Degree Turn and Side Series:

a. Look 270 degrees to the left by turning the head and upper body counterclockwise as much as possible.

b. Turn the right foot in toward the center of the body (pivoting on the heel), shift the weight to the right leg without rising up, and then bring the left foot diagonally forward and across (behind) the back of the right leg to a position that is at approximately 2 o'clock with respect to the right foot.

c. Turn 270 degrees counterclockwise to the left (pivoting on the heel of the right foot and the ball of the left foot) into a left-foot forward Front Stance and do a Lower Block with the left arm as the right hand simultaneously pulls back to chamber (palm up when done) (Fig. 312).

Figure 312

d. Do a Front Snap Kick with the right leg and then return the leg to its starting position in a Front Stance (Fig. 313).

e. Do a right Reverse Punch middle (palm down when done) as the left hand simultaneously pulls back to chamber (palm up when done) (Fig. 314).

Figure 313

f. Circle step forward into a right-foot forward Front Stance and do a left Reverse Punch middle (palm down when done) as the right hand simultaneously pulls back to chamber (palm up when done) (Fig. 315).

Figure 314

Figure 315

9. 180 Degree Turn and Side Series:

   a. Look behind by looking over the right shoulder.

   b. Shift the weight to the left leg without rising up, then put the right foot diagonally behind and to the left of (across) the left leg.

   c. Turn 180 degrees clockwise to the right (pivoting on the heel of the left foot and the ball of the right foot) into a right-foot forward Front Stance and do a Lower Block with the right arm as the left hand simultaneously pulls back to chamber (palm up when done) (Fig. 316).

   d. Do a Front Snap Kick with the left leg and then return the leg to its starting position in a Front Stance (Fig. 317).

   e. Do a left Reverse Punch middle (palm down when done) as the right hand simultaneously pulls back to chamber (palm up when done) (Fig. 318).

   f. Circle step forward into a left foot forward Front Stance and do a right Reverse Punch middle (palm down when done) as the left hand simultaneously pulls back to chamber (palm up when done) (Fig. 319).

Figure 316

Figure 317

Figure 318

Figure 319

10. Recovery — *No-te*

a. Recover by pushing off the left foot and turning 90 degrees counterclockwise to the left and then pushing off the right foot until the body faces the original direction with the feet slightly wider than shoulder width apart.

b. The knees should still be bent and the eyes look to the right (the direction previously faced) the entire time.

c. The arms come to Ready Position (Fig. 320).

d. Stand up slowly while still looking to the right (Fig. 321), then look directly forward (i.e. the direction the body is facing) (Fig. 322).

e. Bring the left foot next to the right foot and bring the arms to the sides of the body (Fig. 323).

f. The *Taikyuku kata* is completed with a bow.

Figure 320

Figure 321

Figure 322

Figure 323

Memory Aids

1. There is a Lower Block on every turn.

2. The Lower Block is done with the arm that is on the same side of the body as the shoulder that is "looked over" before the turn is started.

   If the head is turned counterclockwise and the "look" before the turn is started is over the left shoulder, then the Lower Block will be done with the left arm.

   If the head is turned clockwise and the "look" before the turn is started is over the right shoulder, then the Lower Block will be done with the right arm.

3. On the Side Series, every punch is a middle Reverse Punch with the arm that is on the same side of the body as the back leg of the Front Stance

4. On the Down Center Series, the right arm always punches high and the left arm always punches middle.

5. *Kiai* on the second punch on the third step of the 90 Degree Turn and Down Center Series.

Key Points and Principles for All the Taikyuku Kata

1. Look before starting each turn.

2. All turns pivot on the heel (not the ball) of the back foot.

3. The body should not rise up or drop down during the *kata*.

4. There should be a feeling of driving and pushing off the back leg as a turn is done.

5. When circle stepping forward, the punch starts just as the front foot stops and the knee starts to move forward over the toes.

XIII. Conclusion

By reading this book, you have gained a greater appreciation of Shobayashi Shorin Ryu and Shudokan Karate-do, two classical styles of Okinawan Karate-do and some of the benefits of training in a traditional martial art. You have been introduced to the basic stances, punches, blocks and kicks of Okinawan Karate-do and how to apply these against certain attacks (through the *Ippon Kumite*). I have also explained some traditional exercises to combine these techniques with certain forward and reverse steps (through the *Itosu* and *Kiyan* lines) and multidirectional movements (through the *Taikyuku Kata*).

You must now return to the intersection point at the bottom of the path of interlocking circles and begin again. One must thoroughly know and understand these basics in order to advance to more complex techniques. By continuing to practice and striving for improvement, you will develop body knowledge so that your karate will become your natural reflex. This body knowledge will enable you to intuitively and automatically apply the most appropriate technique at the right time. This is the goal of all martial arts training.

Following the example of Scott Sensei and Sandweiss Sensei, I have also emphasized the principles behind the techniques and exercises in this book. The principles are the key elements which form the essence of effective Okinawan Karate-do. If a particular principle is understood, it may be used to create many techniques and will enhance their effectiveness. The exercises provide a systematic way to practice the techniques and learn how to combine the techniques together. The principles, techniques, and exercises described in this book provide a strong foundation for the development of martial proficiency in karate.

The techniques and exercises must be practiced again and again. It is only with this repeated practice that one can learn and develop the ability to effectively use karate. The journey is not an easy one, but the rewards are substantial. This book will aid you in your own journey of self-development and self-discovery.

APPENDIX A: GLOSSARY

"A" is pronounced like the "a" in Father

"E" is pronounced like the "e" in Ed

"I" is pronounced like the "i" in Police

"O" is pronounced like the "o" in Oats

"U" is pronounced like the "u" in Tune

AGERU UKE (ah-GAIR-roo OO-kay) — Lifting block. A block done by drawing the arm up, slightly across, and in front of the face in a circular motion with the palm facing the body. It starts with the hand at the opposite hip and finishes with the arm above the head (at a 45 degree angle with the palm facing in) and the elbow one fist's width away from the ear.

AIKIDO (eye-KEY-dough) — A Japanese martial art founded by Morihei Ueshiba. Aikido uses primarily joint locks and throwing techniques. Aikido emphasizes blending with opponents and using their energy against them.

BAGUA (BAHG-wah) — A Chinese martial art that is based on the eight trigrams of the *I Ching* (The Book of Changes). Bagua uses circular stepping and emphasizes eight different palm positions. It is considered an "internal" style.

BUDO (BOO-dough) — Literally the "Way of the Warrior." It is also used to refer to traditional Japanese martial arts.

CHI (CHEE) — The Chinese word for the invisible, bioelectric energy that circulates through the body along twelve meridians. Many use the term to describe the life force itself. It is called *ki* in Japanese. It is the basis for acupuncture and acupressure treatments. Chinese martial art styles that emphasize primarily the development and utilization of chi, frequently through softer and slower motions, are referred to as "internal" styles.

CHUDAN UKE (CHEW-don OO-kay) — Middle block. A block done by drawing the arm across the midsection of the body. It starts with the hand at the opposite hip and finishes with the arm (bent at a 90 degree angle) even with the side of the body and the elbow one fist's width away from the ribs.

CHUDAN TSUKI (CHEW-don-tski) — Middle punch. This is generally done so that the hand is directly on the centerline of the body at the level of the solar plexus.

DACHI (DAH-chee) — Literally "to stand," it is used to describe stances.

DAN (DON) — Levels or degrees of black belt. Example: A Sandan is a third degree black belt.

DO (DOUGH) — The "Way" or the "Path" that one follows through life. It is called the *Tao* in Chinese. It is used in the names of many Japanese martial arts to indicate that the practitioners are learning the moral and philosophical aspects of the art in addition to the physical techniques.

DOJO (DOUGH-joe) —A martial arts school. The place where one goes to learn and practice the "Way."

DOSHINKAN (DOUGH-shin-kahn) — The "School of the Way of the Spirit." The name of Grandmaster Isao Ichikawa's style of Shudokan Karate-do. The world headquarters are in Vienna, Austria.

GEDAN BARAI (GAY-don bah-RYE) — Lower block. A block done by bringing the arm down and across the middle and lower sections of the body. It starts with the hand at the opposite ear and finishes with the arm (slightly bent) even with the side of the body and the hand (palm facing in) one fist's width away from the front of the leg.

GERI (GEH-ree) — A kicking technique.

GOJU RYU (go-JEW RYOU) — The Hard/Soft System. An Okinawan style of karate created by Chojun Miyagi. It emphasizes soft, fluid motions and hard motions which incorporate "dynamic breathing." Dynamic breathing involves a tensing of the muscles while coordinating the execution of the technique with a slow, forced exhale. One of the two main systems of Okinawan Karate-do. It is also known as Naha-te (the hands of the city of Naha) and Higashionna-ha (the system of Higashionna).

GYAKU TSUKI (GYAH-coo tski) — Reverse punch. A punch done with the arm on the same side of the body as the back leg (generally in a Front Stance). It is also frequently used to describe punches where the forearm rotates so that the palm of the punching fist faces down (toward the ground) when the punch is completed.

GOSHIN JUTSU (GO-shin ji-TSUE) — The Japanese name for all self-defense systems that are primarily designed for combat purposes and do not fall within the category of traditional or classical martial arts.

HACHIJI DACHI (hah-CHEE-jee DAH-chee) — Open leg or natural stance. An upright stance with the heels of the feet shoulder width apart and the feet turned outward at a 45 degree angle.

HAJIME (hah-ji-MEH) — Start or begin.

HEIKO DACHI (HEY-co DAH-chee) — Parallel stance. An upright stance with the heels of the feet shoulder width apart and the feet parallel to each other.

HEISOKU DACHI (hey-S0-coo DAH-chee) — Informal attention stance with feet straight. An upright stance with the feet together and the back straight.

HOMBU DOJO (HOM-boo DOUGH-joe) — The headquarter martial arts school.

HSING-YI (SHING-ee) —A Chinese martial art that is based on the principles of the Law of Five Elements. The five elements are fire, metal, wood, water, and earth.

IAIDO (ee-EYE-dough) — A Japanese martial art that specializes in drawing the sword and cutting quickly and effectively. The original goal was to be able to kill an opponent immediately after drawing the sword with only a single stroke.

IPPON KUMITE (ee-PON COO-me-teh) — One-step fighting or sparring. It is frequently used to describe any two-person exercise that involves a prearranged sequence with only a single attack.

ISSHIN RYU (ISH-shin RYOU) — The One Heart Style. The name of an Okinawan style of karate that was formed by Tatsuo Shimabuku by combining techniques from the Shorin Ryu and Goju Ryu systems of Okinawan Karate-do.

ITOSU LINES (ee-TOE-sue) — Line drills from the Shorin Ryu system that emphasize turning the hips to generate greater power in one's punches, blocks, and kicks. It is believed that these were created by Yasutsune Itosu, a famous Okinawan teacher and practitioner of Okinawan Karate-do.

JODAN UKE (JOE-don OO-kay) — Upper block. A block done as though punching something directly above the ear on the opposite side of the body. It finishes with the arm above the head (at a 45 degree angle with the palm facing out) and the elbow one fist's width away from the ear.

JUDO (JEW-dough) — The Way of Flexibility. A Japanese martial art founded by Jigoro Kano. Judo uses primarily grappling and throwing techniques.

KAGI TSUKI (KAH-gee-tski) — Hooking punch.

KAMAE (kah-MY) — A pause that occurs when the hands are in a resting or fixed position.

KAMAE-TE (kah-MY teh) — To put one's hands in a formal ready position. It is similar to the expression "On Guard" used in European swordsmanship.

KARATE (ca-RAH-teh) — Empty hand. It was originally spelled with the Japanese character for China which is pronounced the same as the character for empty. Karate (China hand) was used to describe fighting techniques and systems that the Okinawans originally learned through trading with the Chinese. It is also used to describe fighting systems that primarily emphasize punching, striking, kicking, and blocking techniques.

KARATE-DO (ca-RAH-teh-dough) — The Way of the Empty Hand.

KATA (KAH-tah) — The formal name for prearranged sequences or forms comprised of various blocks, punches, kicks and stances designed to teach and improve one's fighting skills. Many kata have been passed down from teachers to students for hundreds of years.

KENDO (KEN-dough) — The Way of the Sword. A Japanese martial art that teaches swordsmanship primarily through practice with *bokken* (wooden swords), *shinai* (bamboo swords), and body armor.

KI (KEY) — The Japanese word for the invisible, bioelectric energy that circulates through the body along twelve meridians. Many use the term to describe the life force itself. It is called *chi* in Chinese. It is the basis for acupuncture and acupressure treatments. The development and utilization of ki is a part of all traditional Japanese martial arts, but some systems like Aikido place a greater emphasis on its use.

KIAI (key-EYE) — Literally the "union of energy." In martial arts, it means to project your energy or spirit. It is a technique used to increase the power and effectiveness of a strike. It is also used to describe the loud shouts done with certain attacks.

KIBA DACHI (KEY-bah DAH-chee) — Horse stance. The feet are parallel and approximately two shoulder (or hip) widths apart with the knees pushed out and over the toes.

KIOTSUKI (key-OH-tsuske) — The command to line up or come to attention.

KIRITSU (key-REE-tsue) — The command to return to a standing position from *seiza* (formal kneeling position).

KIYAN LINES (KEY-on) — Line drills from the Shorin Ryu system that emphasize moving forward and backward in a front stance. It is believed that these were created by Master Chotoku Kiyan, a famous Okinawan teacher and practitioner of Okinawan Karate-do. Master Kiyan was Grandmaster Eizo Shimabukuro's primary teacher and role model. He was also the founder of the Shobayashi branch of Shorin Ryu.

KODOKAN JUDO (co-DOUGH-kahn JEW-dough) — The headquarters school where Grandmaster Jigaro Kano, the founder of Judo, taught classes. It is also used to refer to Grandmaster Kano's style of Judo.

KO-TAI (CO-tie) — Switch or change.

KOKUSAI BUDOIN (COKE-sigh boo-DOUGH-in) — A martial arts federation that was formed in 1952 to foster the promotion of friendship and cooperation among practitioners of traditional Japanese martial arts. Kokusai Budoin means "International Martial Arts Federation" in English. The official name is "Kokusai Budoin — International Martial Arts Federation."

KUNG FU (KUNG (or GUNG) FOO) — The Chinese character means "hard work." It is also used to refer to Chinese martial arts.

KYOSHI (KYO-she) — A samurai title which is awarded to recognize an individual's accomplishments in the martial arts. It means "Full Professor" or "Teaching Model" and is comparable to the title of *Shihan*.

KYU (CUE) — Levels or degrees below black belt. Ex: An Ikyu is one level below blackbelt. A Rhokukyu is six levels below black belt.

MAE GERI (MY-eh GEH-ree) — Front kick.

MAKIWARA (mah-KEY-wah-reh) — A training device created by Okinawans. It was generally a chest-high post which was embedded in the ground to provide resistance for punching and kicking practice as well as to toughen various parts of the body. The striking surface was originally padded with sheaved rice straw.

MAWATE (mah-WAH-teh) — The command to turn.

MAWASHI GERI (mah-WAH-she GEH-ree) — Roundhouse kick.

MAWASHI TSUKI (mah-WAH-she-tski) — Roundhouse punch.

MEIJIN (MAY-gin) — A samurai title which is awarded to recognize an individual's accomplishments in the martial arts. It means "Grandmaster" and is the highest title awarded by Kokusai Budoin.

MOKUSO (moak-SO) — To meditate.

MOROTE TSUKI (moe-ROE-teh tski) — Double punch.

MUSUBI DACHI (moo-SUE-bee DAH-chee) — Informal attention stance with feet out. An upright stance with the heels together and the feet turned outward at a 45 degree angle.

NEKO-ASHI DACHI (NEH-co-ah-she DAH-chee) — Cat stance. A stance where 90 percent of the weight is on the back leg (which is bent as much as possible with the foot turned outward at a 45 degree angle) and the hips are shifted back. The front foot rests lightly on the ball of the foot. It should be approximately one foot in front of the other foot and the inside edges of the feet are on either side of a line coming straight forward.

NIDAN (NEE-don) — Second step or level. It may also refer to a 2nd degree blackbelt.

NIHON JUJUTSU (nee-HOHN jew-ji-TSUE) — Japanese Jujutsu. Jujutsu is a very old martial art that emphasizes joint locks and throwing techniques.

NO-TE (NO-teh) — To return one's hands (and body) to a ready position.

NUKITE (new-KEY-teh) — Spear hand. A punch done with the fingers extended and together.

OI TSUKI (OI tski) — Lunge punch. A punch done with the arm on the same side of the body as the front leg (generally in a Front Stance).

OKINAWA (o-key-NAH-wah) — A small island (10 miles by 30 miles) off the coast of Japan. It is the birth place of karate which developed as a result of the combination of indigenous fighting systems and Chinese martial arts.

O KUGE (o COO-geh) — Innermost secrets and techniques.

REI (RAY) — The command to execute a bow.

RENSHI (WREN-she) — A samurai title which is awarded to recognize an individual's accomplishments in the martial arts. It means "Assistant Professor" or "Expert."

SANDAN (SAHN-don) — Third step or level. It may also refer to a 3rd degree blackbelt.

SEIZA (SAY-zah) — A way of sitting on your heels that is the typical way Japanese sit on the ground. In martial arts it is used as a formal kneeling position.

SENSEI (SEN-say) — Literally one who was "born before." It is used to describe, name or address a teacher.

SHAOLIN (SHAOW-lynn) — The name of a Buddhist temple in China that became famous for the martial arts it developed. It is believed to be the birth place of most Chinese, Japanese and Korean martial art systems.

SHIBUCHO (SHE-boo-choe) — Director or superintendent. The title given to someone who is put in charge of a particular region or area. In a military situation, it would be similar to a field appointment of a lower ranking soldier to the level of general for a particular assignment or region.

SHIHAN (SHE-hahn) — A samurai title which is awarded to recognize an individual's accomplishments in the martial arts. It means "Full Professor" or "Teaching Model" and is comparable to the title of *Kyoshi*.

SHIHANCHI (SHE-hahn-chee) — A samurai title which means protege.

SHIKO DACHI (SHE-co DAH-chee) — Sumo stance. The feet are turned outward at a 45 degree angle and the heels are approximately two shoulder (or hip) widths apart with the knees pushed out.

SHOBAYASHI SHORIN RYU (show-buy-AH-she SHOW-rin RYOU) — The "Small Forest" style of Okinawan Karate-do that was taught by Grandmaster Chotoku Kiyan. The current Grandmaster is Eizo Shimabukuro.

SHODAN (SHOW-don) — First level or step. It is also used to refer to a 1st-degree blackbelt.

SHORIN RYU (SHOW-rin RYOU) — The Young Forest Style. One of the two main systems of Okinawan karate. It is also known as Okinawa-te (the hands of Okinawa), Shuri-te (the hands of the city of Shuri), and Itosu-ha (the system of Itosu).

SHOTOKAN (SHOW-toe-kahn) — A Japanese style of karate that was created by Master Gichin Funakoshi. Master Funakoshi was the first person to demonstrate and teach karate in Japan. He is largely responsible for the popularity of karate in the world today.

SHUDOKAN (shoe-DOUGH-kahn) — The Institute for the Cultivation of the Way. A Japanese style of Okinawan karate that was created by Master Kanken Toyama, an Okinawan karate master.

SHUTO UKE (SHOE-toe OO-kay) — Knife-hand or sword-hand block.

SHUTO-URA UKE (SHOE-toe U-rah OO-kay) — Circle block. A block done by bringing the arm (with the fingers extended and together) up in front of the face and then back down to the side of the body in an elliptical pathway. It starts like an Upper Block, goes through its elliptical pathway, and finishes with the arm (bent at a 90 degree angle and the palm facing away from the body) even with the side of the body and the elbow one fist's width away from the ribs. This block may also be done at a lower level to protect the mid-section of the body.

SIFU (SEE-foo) — The Chinese word for teacher.

SIL-LUM HUNG-GAR KUNG FU (SEAL-lum HUNG-gar KUNG [*or* GUNG] FOO) — The Shaolin Tiger-Crane System of Kung Fu. A Chinese martial art that emphasizes techniques that imitate the movements and fighting styles of tigers and cranes.

SO-SHIHAN (SO-she-hahn) — A samurai title which is awarded to recognize an individual's accomplishments in the martial arts. It means "Chief Professor" or "Chief Teaching Model."

SOTO SEIKEN UKE (SO-toe SAY-ken OO-kay) — Cross block. A block done by driving the arm across the midsection of the body along a trajectory that is at a 45 degree angle to the chest. It starts with the hand at the shoulder and finishes with the arm bent at a 90 degree angle, the hand directly in front of the opposite shoulder, and the elbow one fist's width away from the solar plexus. This block may also be done at a higher level to protect the face.

TAIKYUKU (tie-CUE-coo) — Basic training *kata* from the Shudokan system which emphasize getting power from the legs and hips. The name means "first cause" or the first kata that one learns.

TAE KWON DO (TIE KWAHN dough) — A Korean style of karate created in the 20th century.

T'AI CHI CH'UAN (TIE CHEE CHWAN) — "Supreme Ultimate Fist or Boxing." A Chinese martial art that emphasizes slow, fluid motions while being rooted to the ground. Relaxation and the integration of the mind and body with slow, even breathing are also emphasized. In addition to being an effective martial art, it is also widely practiced for the health benefits that come from learning to circulate one's *chi* and the meditative aspects of concentrated practice.

TANG SOO DO (TANG SUE DOUGH) — A traditional Korean style of karate.

TATE TSUKI (TAH-teh-tski) — Vertical punch.

TE (TEH) — Hand or hands. It is also used to refer to types of Okinawan martial arts. For example, Shorin Ryu is also known as Okinawa-te.

TORI (TOR-ree) — One who is the "doer." In grappling arts, the tori is the one who does the throw or technique.

TOMARI-TE (toe-MAR-ree-teh) — Originally one of the three main systems of Okinawan karate, it is now extinct except to the extent its *kata* have been absorbed and preserved in the Shorin Ryu and Goju Ryu systems.

TSUKI (TSKI) — A punch.

UCHI-HACHIJI DACHI (OO-chee hah-CHEE-jee DAH-chee) — Inverted open-leg stance. The heels of the feet are shoulder width apart and the feet are turned inward (pigeon-toed) at a 45 degree angle with the hips tucked upward.

UKE (OO-kay) — A block or one who is the defender.

UKEMI (oo-KEM-ee) — Falling techniques and absorption. A generic term used to describe techniques such as rolls and breakfalls which are the safest way to land when one is thrown to the ground.

URA TSUKI (U-rah-tski) — A punch done with the palm facing up.

USHIRO GERI (oo-SHEAR-roe GEH-ree) — Back kick.

WADO-RYU (wah-DOUGH-RYOU) — An Okinawan style of karate founded by Grandmaster Hironishi Ohtsuka, a Kokusai Budoin Meijin.

WING CHUN KUNG FU (WING CHUN KUNG [or GUNG] FOO) — A Chinese martial art that emphasizes straight-line attacks along the centerline and sticking/maintaining contact with an opponent's arms and legs.

WUSHU (WOO-shoe) — The generic term for Chinese martial arts.

YAME (yah-MEH) — The command to stop or finish.

YOI (YOI) — The command to assume a ready position.

YOKO GERI (YOE-co GEH-ree) — Side kick.

ZEN KUTSU DACHI (ZEN COOT-sue DAH-chee) — Front stance. The front leg is bent with the knee pushed forward over the toes and the back leg is straight and extended to the rear. Sixty percent of the weight is on the front leg. The back foot is turned outward at a 45 degree angle and the front foot points straight forward. The width of the stance is shoulder (or hip, if wider) width apart and the hips and shoulders are square to the front.

NUMBERS

ICHI (EE-chee) — One

NI (nee) — Two

SAN (sahn) — Three

SHI or YON (she) or (yon) — Four

GO (go) — Five

RHOKU (ROW-coo) — Six

SHICHI (SHE-chee) — Seven

HACHI (HAH-chee) — Eight

KU (coo) — Nine

JU (jew) — Ten

NIJU (NEE-jew) — Twenty

NIJU-ICH (NEE-jew-eech) — Twenty-one

SANJU (SAHN-jew) — Thirty

YONJU (YAHN-jew) — Forty

GOJU (GO-jew) — Fifty

RHOKUJU (ROW-coo-jew) — Sixty

SHICHIJU (SHE-chee-jew) — Seventy

HACHIJU (HAH-chee-jew) — Eighty

KUJU (COO-jew) — Ninety

HYAKU (HYAH-coo) — One Hundred

NI-HYAKU NIJU-ICH (NEE-hyah-coo NEE-jew-eech) — Two Hundred Twenty-one

RANKS ABOVE BLACKBELT

SHODAN (SHOW-dan) — First degree blackbelt

NIDAN (NEE-don) — Second degree blackbelt

SANDAN (SAHN-don) — Third degree blackbelt

YONDAN (YON-don) — Fourth degree blackbelt

GODAN (GO-don) — Fifth degree blackbelt

RHOKUDAN (ROW-coo-don) — Sixth degree blackbelt

SHICHIDAN (SHE-chee-don) — Seventh degree blackbelt

HACHIDAN (HAH-chee-don) — Eighth degree blackbelt

KUDAN (COO-don) — Ninth degree blackbelt

JUDAN (JEW-don) — Tenth degree blackbelt or redbelt

RANKS BELOW BLACKBELT

JUKYU (JEW-cue) — Tenth level (White belt level)

KUKYU (COO-cue) — Ninth level (White belt level)

HACHIKYU (HAH-chee-CUE) — Eighth level (White belt level)

SHICHIKYU (SHE-chee-cue) — Seventh level (White belt level)

RHOKUKYU (ROW-coo-cue) — Sixth level (Green belt level)

GOKYU (GO-cue) — Fifth level (Green belt level)

YONKYU (YON-cue) — Fourth level (Green belt level)

SANKYU (SAHN-cue) — Third level (Brown belt level)

NIKYU (NEE-cue) — Second level (Brown belt level)

IKYU (EE-cue) — First level (Brown belt level)

APPENDIX B: INDEX

APPENDIX C: SHORT DESCRIPTION REFERENCE SECTION

Short Descriptions of the Itosu Lines

Itosu Shodan

1. Moving Forward:

   a. Do the Opening for the *Itosu* lines.

   b. Do a Circle Block with the left arm as the right hand pulls back to chamber (palm up when done). The left fingers squeeze into a fist as though grabbing another person's sleeve. The hips and shoulders rotate counterclockwise as the right hand does a middle Reverse Punch (palm down when done) as the left hand simultaneously pulls back to chamber (palm up when done) (Fig. 324).

   c. On subsequent steps forward, rotate the hips and shoulders as one unit and do a middle Reverse Punch (palm down when done) with the hand that is on the same side of the body as the back leg of the *Itosu* Stance. The other hand simultaneously pulls back to chamber (palm up when done).

2. Moving Back:

   a. Step straight back into a Cat Stance. Do a Middle Block with the arm on the same side of the body as the front leg of the Cat Stance. The other hand simultaneously pulls back to chamber (palm up when done) (Fig. 325).

Figure 324

Figure 325

Itosu Nidan

1. Moving Forward:

   a. This is the same as Moving Forward for *Itosu Shodan* except the Reverse Punch (palm down when done) is a High Punch (Fig. 326).

Figure 326

2. Moving Back:

   a. On the first series only, step straight back into a Cat Stance and pull the hands back into a *kamae* at chamber. A *kamae* is a pause that occurs when the hands are in a resting or fixed position. The palms should be facing each other on the same side of the body as the front leg of the Cat Stance. The palm of the hand that punched last faces up and is underneath the other hand (Fig. 327). The arm with the hand facing up does a middle level Cross Block as the other hand pulls back to chamber (palm up when done) (Fig. 328). The arm that just did the Cross Block then does a Lower Block (Fig. 329).

   b. On subsequent steps, there is no *kamae*. After the step back, the arm with the hand at chamber position does a middle level Cross Block as the other hand pulls back to chamber (palm up when done). The arm that just did the Cross Block then does a Lower Block.

Figure 327

Figure 328

Figure 329

Itosu Sandan

1. Moving Forward:

   a. Do the Opening for the *Itosu* lines.

   b. Without twisting the hips, do an Upper Block with the arm that is on the same side of the body as the front leg of the *Itosu* Stance. The other hand simultaneously pulls back to chamber (palm up when done) (Fig. 330).

2. Moving Back:

   a. Step straight back into a Cat Stance. Do a Lifting Block with the arm on the same side of the body as the front leg of the Cat Stance. The other hand simultaneously pulls back to chamber (palm up when done) (Fig. 331).

Figure 330

Figure 331

Short Descriptions of the Kiyan Lines

Kiyan Shodan

1. Moving Forward:

   a. Do the Opening for *Kiyan Shodan* and *Kiyan Nidan*.

   b. Circle step forward into a Front Stance and do a middle Lunge Punch (palm down when done) with the hand on the same side of the body as the front leg of the Front Stance. The other hand simultaneously pulls back to chamber (palm up when done) (Fig. 332).

2. Moving Back:

   a. Circle step backward into a Front Stance and pull the hands back into a *kamae* at chamber (with palms facing each other) on the same side of the body as the back leg of the Front Stance. (The palm of the hand that is on the same side of the body as the back leg of the Front Stance faces up and that hand is underneath the other hand) (Fig. 333)

   b. Do a Middle Block with the arm that is on the same side of the body as the front leg of the Front Stance. The blocking arm stays in the Middle Block position while the other hand does a Reverse Punch middle (palm down when done) (Fig. 334).

Figure 332

Figure 333

Figure 334

Kiyan Nidan

1. Moving Forward:

   a. This is the same as Moving Forward for *Kiyan Shodan* except the Lunge Punch (palm down when done) is a High Punch (Fig. 335).

2. Moving Back:

   a. Circle step backward into a Front Stance and pull the hands back into a *kamae* position at chamber (with palms facing up) on the same side of the body as the back leg of the Front Stance. (The hand that is on the same side of the body as the back leg of the Front Stance is underneath the other hand.) (Fig. 336) Do an Upper Block with the arm that is on the same side of the body as the front leg of the Front Stance. The blocking arm stays in the Upper Block position while the other hand does a Reverse Punch high (palm down when done) (Fig. 337).

Figure 335

Figure 336

Figure 337

Kiyan Sandan

1. Moving Forward:

   a. Bow. Step out into Ready Position.

   b. Step forward with the left foot and go down onto the right knee. (The right foot should be on the ball of the foot.) Do a Lower Block (which stops directly above the left knee) with the left arm. The right hand simultaneously pulls back to chamber (palm up when done) (Fig. 338).

Figure 338

   c. The right hand does a Reverse Punch (palm down when done) to the height of the solar plexus while on one knee. The left hand simultaneously pulls back to chamber (palm up when done) (Fig. 339). Stand up (moving forward) using both legs equally.

2. Moving Back:

   a. Step backward with the right foot and go down onto the right knee. (The right foot should be on the ball of the foot.) Do a *Shuto* Block (an openhanded Lower Block which stops directly above the left knee) with the left arm. The right hand simultaneously pulls back to chamber in a fist (palm up when done) (Fig. 340).

Figure 339

   b. The right hand (with fingers together and extended) does a *nukite* thrust (a spear-hand thrust with the thumb-side up) to the height of the solar plexus while on one knee. The left hand simultaneously pulls back to chamber in a fist (palm up when done) (Fig. 341). Stand up (moving backward) using both legs equally.

Figure 340

Figure 341

Short Descriptions of the Taikyuku Kata

Taikyuku Shodan

1. Side Series:

    a. Do a Lower Block on the turn with the arm that is on the same side of the body as the front leg of the Front Stance (after the turn is completed) as the other hand simultaneously pulls back to chamber (palm up when done) (Fig. 342).

    b. After the turn, circle step forward into a Front Stance and do a middle Lunge Punch (palm down when done) with the arm that is on the same side of the body as the front leg of the Front Stance (after the step forward is completed) as the other hand simultaneously pulls back to chamber (palm up when done) (Fig. 343).

Figure 342

Figure 343

2. Down Center Series:

    a. Do a Lower Block on the turn with the left arm as the right hand pulls back to chamber (palm up when done) (Fig. 344).

    b. After the turn, circle step forward into a Front Stance three times and on each step do a middle Lunge Punch (palm down when done) with the arm that is on the same side of the body as the front leg of the Front Stance (after the step forward is completed) as the other hand pulls back to chamber (palm up when done) (Fig. 345). *Kiai* on the third punch.

3. Memory Aids

    a. There is a Lower Block on every turn.

    b. The Lower Block is done with the arm that is on the same side of the body as the shoulder that is "looked over" before the turn is started.

    If the head is turned counterclockwise and the "look" before the turn is started is over the left shoulder, then the Lower Block will be done with the left arm.

    If the head is turned clockwise and the "look" before the turn is started is over the right shoulder, then the Lower Block will be done with the right arm.

    c. Every punch is a middle Lunge Punch with the arm that is on the same side of the body as the front leg of the Front Stance.

    d. *Kiai* on the third punch of the Down Center Series.

Figure 344

Figure 345

Taikyuku Nidan

1. Side Series:

   a. Do a Middle Block on the turn with the arm that is on the same side of the body as the front leg of the Front Stance (after the turn is completed) as the other hand pulls back to chamber (palm up when done) (Fig. 346).

   b. After the turn, circle step forward into a Front Stance and do an Upper Block with the arm that is on the same side of the body as the front leg of the Front Stance (after the step forward is completed) as the other hand pulls back to chamber (palm up when done) (Fig. 347). Do a Reverse Punch middle (palm down when done) with the arm that is on the same side of the body as the back leg of the Front Stance as the other hand pulls back to chamber (palm up when done) (Fig. 348).

Figure 346

Figure 347

Figure 348

2. Down Center Series:

   a. Do a Lower Block on the turn with the left arm as the right hand pulls back to chamber (palm up when done) (Fig. 349). Do a right Reverse Punch middle (palm down when done) as the left hand pulls back to chamber (palm up when done) (Fig. 350).

   b. After the punch, circle step forward into a Front Stance three times and on each step do a Reverse Punch middle (palm down when done) with the arm that is on the same side of the body as the back leg of the Front Stance (after the step forward is completed) as the other hand pulls back to chamber (palm up when done) (Fig. 351). *Kiai* on the punch on the third step forward.

3. Memory Aids

   a. The Middle Block or Lower Block on the turns is done with the arm that is on the same side of the body as the shoulder that is "looked over" before the turn is started.

   If the head is turned counterclockwise and the "look" before the turn is started is over the left shoulder, then the Middle Block or Lower Block will be done with the left arm.

   If the head is turned clockwise and the "look" before the turn is started is over the right shoulder, then the Middle Block or Lower Block will be done with the right arm.

   b. Every punch is a middle Reverse Punch with the arm that is on the same side of the body as the back leg of the Front Stance.

   c. *Kiai* on the punch on the third step of the Down Center Series.

Figure 349

Figure 350

Figure 351

Taikyuku Sandan

1. Side Series:

   a. Do a Lower Block on the turn with the arm that is on the same side of the body as the front leg of the Front Stance (after the turn is completed) as the other hand pulls back to chamber (palm up when done) (Fig. 352). Do a Front Snap Kick with the leg that is on the same side of the body as the back leg of the Front Stance and then return the leg to its starting position in a Front Stance (Fig. 353). Do a Reverse Punch middle (palm down when done) with the arm that is on the same side of the body as the back leg of the Front Stance as the other hand pulls back to chamber (palm up when done) (Fig. 354).

   b. After the punch, circle step forward into a Front Stance and do a Reverse Punch middle (palm down when done) with the arm that is on the same side of the body as the back leg of the Front Stance (after the step forward is completed) as the other hand pulls back to chamber (palm up when done) (Fig. 355).

Figure 352

Figure 353

Figure 354

Figure 355

2. Down Center Series:

     a. Do a Lower Block on the turn with the left arm as the right hand pulls back to chamber (palm up when done) (Fig. 356).

     b. After the turn, circle step forward into a Front Stance three times and on each step do a right punch high (palm down when done) as the left hand pulls back to chamber (palm up when done) (Fig. 357) and then do a Left Punch middle (palm down when done) as the right hand pulls back to chamber (palm up when done) (Fig. 358). *Kiai* on the second punch on the third step forward.

3. Memory Aids

     a. There is a Lower Block on every turn.

Figure 356

     b. The Lower Block is done with the arm that is on the same side of the body as the shoulder that is "looked over" before the turn is started.

     If the head is turned counterclockwise and the "look" before the turn is started is over the left shoulder, then the Lower Block will be done with the left arm.

     If the head is turned clockwise and the "look" before the turn is started is over the right shoulder, then the Lower Block will be done with the right arm.

     c. On the side series, every punch is a middle Reverse Punch with the arm that is on the same side of the body as the back leg of the Front Stance.

     d. On the Down Center Series, the right arm always punches high and the left arm always punches middle.

Figure 357

     e. *Kiai* on the second punch on the third step of the Down Center Series.

Figure 358

APPENDIX D: SAMPLE WORKOUT

A. Warm-ups

B. Punches

1. Punch for form, power, and speed (two punches) in a Horse Stance, Front Stance, and Cat Stance

2. Punching Drill

C. Blocks

1. Upper Block, Middle Block, Cross Block, Lower Block, Circle Block, and Lifting Block

2. Blocking Drill — Start with the right hand and do two of each block in the order listed above.

D. Kicks

1. Front Kick

2. Side Kick

3. Roundhouse Kick

4. Back Kick

E. Line Drills

1. *Itosu* Lines

   a. Practice stepping alone

   b. *Itosu Shodan*

   c. *Itosu Nidan*

   d. *Itosu Sandan*

2. *Kiyan* Lines

   a. Practice stepping alone

   b. *Kiyan Shodan*

   c. *Kiyan Nidan*

   d. *Kiyan Sandan*

F. Taikyuku Kata

1. Practice Stepping Alone

2. *Taikyuku Shodan*

3. *Taikyuku Nidan*

4. *Taikyuku Sandan*

G. Two-Person Exercises (Individual Practice)

1. High — Middle — Low

2. Singles, Doubles, and Triples

3. Lower Series

4. If a partner is not available, practice the moves alone for both the Attacker and the Defender. This will help the body learn and internalize the specific movements of the different exercises. When the exercises are later done with a partner, more attention can be placed on interacting with the partner instead of on remembering the movements of the exercise. Individual practice of the Two-Person Exercises can also significantly increase speed because there is no waiting for an attack or counter.

Look for these other great Masters Press titles!